ABOUT THE AUTHOR

Donald W. Bartow is a graduate of Findlay College, attended Bowling Green State University, and was educated in theology at Winebrenner School of Theology. After serving in several pastorates in Ohio, he came to his present position, pastor of the Westminster United Presbyterian Church of Canton, Ohio.

Creative
Churchmanship

Donald W. Bartow

Creative
Churchmanship

 The World Publishing Company
NEW YORK AND CLEVELAND

Published by The World Publishing Company
2231 West 110th Street, Cleveland, Ohio 44102
Published simultaneously in Canada by
Nelson, Foster & Scott Ltd.

First Printing—1969

WORLD PUBLISHING
    TIMES MIRROR

Grateful acknowledgment is made to
The National Church Supply Company, Chester, West Virginia,
for their permission to reproduce the copyrighted
forms and records appearing in this book.

Preface

Today there is a burning desire on the part of many to break from the Institutional Church. They are convinced they can better serve God and man by so doing. The coffeehouse, attic, listening post, small group, spiritual personality development groups, etc., may be stimulating, but they are not the avenue of religious contact for most people. The great majority of religious individuals of this generation and of the generations that lie ahead will experience the impact of faith from the Institutional Church.

Unique ministries develop because of the Institutional Church and not in spite of it. Minus the institution with all of its frailties, splinter groups and movements could never exist. They are merely accented emphases upon a particular effort or experience. They concentrate on a single problem or doctrine and do so to the neglect of many other equally deserving concerns. The purpose of this book is to face the fact that the Institutional Church and its parish programing are still with us and will continue to be with us in the future. The local parish plan is not about to be doomed to destruction or discarded.

Once we face the fact that the Institutional Church is with us we can move ahead to creative churchmanship and the whys and hows of such an approach.

Church renewal is a popular phrase today. It implies

that a condition once existed which then waned or changed and which can now be recaptured. It insists that there is a possibility, however remote, for an individual or institution to return to a vitality once experienced. This concept alone falls far short of the Church's need in our generation. Frankly, to what age, generation, year, or structure would the Church want to return? Would it wish to become again the Church of the early thirties, the turn-of-the-century Church, the medieval Church, or even the first-century Church? Would we want the Corinthian Church of Paul's day? I believe that thoughtful individuals will agree that none of these periods could serve as the yardstick for measuring church vitality. There is no particular age to which we can, or should desire to, return.

Granted, we need renewal at all times; but more than this, we need rebirth. The Church needs to be revived in those areas of worship that have proved helpful through the ages. But, it must come alive also in new areas. In every aspect, the present generation must be born into the Kingdom of God. An awakening must lead us to an awareness of the God of history speaking and permeating every facet of individual life and of society.

Many men of the past journeyed by faith into unknown realms. Abraham moved to a strange country; Moses entered uncharted wilderness with thousands of displaced persons; Nicodemus advanced to a concept of faith beyond his comprehension. God never asked these leaders to return to the past. God inspired their trust and led them into the future. This is faith.

Creative churchmanship involves walking by faith. It lets the past speak to us, but not suppress us. It entails living in the present and facing the future with courage. Such is the spirit that can and must indwell the Institutional Church.

Thank God for the many who seek guidance and support

in experiencing the desired new birth. They deserve an apology for faltering leadership, often within the Church itself. The Church states problems, but offers no solutions. It gives great spiritual admonition in general terms, but lacks specific examples and guidance. Churchmen are polished experts in the not-so-gentle art of criticizing, and clumsy beginners in leading the way. It is easy to catalog the wrongs of the Church, but difficult to set forth suggestions whereby it can witness effectively in this critical hour.

Our immediate concern is to set forth guidelines for an awakened ministry on the part of both laity and clergy. Every believer is a minister; the professional clergy are but a small percentage of those who have confessed faith in the Lord Jesus Christ. The Church's ministers number in the millions, and each of us must make the most of our ministry.

We do not evangelize when we guess at people's needs. We must identify with their needs and meet them at their level of understanding. To use the institution as an excuse not to get involved is possible. And the institution will shrivel to a spiritual stalemate. But the institution can also inspire us and can serve as a bulwark in maintaining vision and vitality to minister to all. We must make the choice.

Will we destroy the institution or will we permit it to redeem us? Will we always be lamenting the many problems and shortcomings of the institution, or will we stir our own hearts and souls as the great teachings of the Church speak?

No book can ever hope to present all facets of new life in the Church. But I hope that some will be helped and all will be encouraged through the limited comments and suggestions of this one. Of course I do not claim that the ideas and suggestions of this book are the only way to new life in the Church. A useful and redemptive purpose will be served if my suggestions can in any way guide church programing and action.

7

Contents

Creative
Churchmanship

One

Nudged by
the Negative

Christ said, "Go ye into all the world and preach the Gospel to every creature." The Divine directive has never been rescinded. The Church has its marching orders and dare not sound retreat. There is no other way than forward with Christ.

The population explosion threatens and challenges the Church. Either there will be more millions won to Christ or the ranks of the unbelievers will reach staggering proportions and virtually black out the impact of the Church in the world. The Christian Church started as a minority movement. If present trends continue, it will not be long until once again believers will constitute but a very small percentage of the world's people.

Countries that are not predominantly Christian have experienced the greatest population increases. This is one challenge to the Church. In addition, millions are outside the Church even in so-called Christian nations. In America today are people who have not heard of Christ, and of those who have, most have not made a life-commitment to Him. The field of evangelism is thus not only ripe unto harvest in the

Church's neighborhood, but also in the nave of the churches. Reapers are needed.

Decreasing participation in the life of the Institutional Church is alarming. Sunday church school, worship attendance, midweek service, and Sunday night meetings have in many congregations witnessed a sharp decline in attendance. This slump is a warning signal. It is readily admitted that such services are not necessarily "sacred" and that they are not the sole criterion of life in the Church. Other ways may be found for expressing one's faith and communal fellowship. If so, the Church must soon discover them and incorporate them into its life, perhaps eliminating some of the present stereotyped services. Many church meetings in their present format are not serving today's needs. New life must be breathed into them or new forms must replace them that will instruct and inspire individuals to commitment to Christ.

A post-mortem cannot restore life, but it can impart information for treating the living. Examination of some Church practices may reveal one or more causes of the death of vital Church life. Too often, creative concern and outreach have been neglected to the critical stage where life slowly but surely departed.

Attendance Only

Motivation directed solely toward increasing attendance at church school or Sunday morning worship is certainly an unworthy reflection on personal concern or depth evangelism. Contests, gimmicks, and public relations drives may increase attendance in church services and church-related activities, but this does not mean that souls have been awakened to Christ. Frequently, in sections of the country where church attendance is highest, leadership is often indifferent to the real issues of the day. Merely attending church can be a hindrance, rather than a help, in ministering "unto the least of these my brethren."

Cleaning the Rolls

Some hold that evangelism can be given a shot in the arm through the efforts of "dedicated" members who would weed out the rolls of inactive members. They feel that their church will be made more pure and powerful when it is purged of the inactive. In other words, the inference is that the "active" have accepted the challenge and call of Christ; the "inactive" have rejected the faith within their hearts, and do not express the faith in their daily lives. Local church leaders sometimes fail to appreciate that inactive individuals may be doing the Kingdom of God a favor. At the least, they are not abetting some of the asinine efforts that churches attempt to promote and to perpetuate. Churches have certain building programs and emphases that cause their people to sin as they are cajoled, threatened, and challenged to support them. Cleaning the rolls of individuals not willing to support programs of dubious value is an ineffective way to gain the world for Christ. The indifference of so many may be the strongest voice in the Church, crying out to it that its programs need to become more vital.

Reactivation

Another faulty emphasis in evangelism is the attempt to reactivate the inactive despite existing and often inadequate programs. Some feel that if they make enough calls and are "really friendly," the Kingdom will come to all. Friendship has merit, but many of the programs designed to reactivate lapsed members are so puerile that the inactive can hardly be blamed for not responding and returning to services. Evangelism based only upon friendliness is virtually destined to failure, and thank God this is so. If the inactivity resulted from a poor church program, then returning to more of the same will prove unfruitful.

Financially Solvent

There are members of every church who believe that only when people are present at services will they contribute. The conclusion is that offerings are down because of people absent. If no strong effort is made to keep individuals enthused, then too few are left to pay all the bills. Like it or not, much emphasis is put upon the thesis that church members should give regardless of the programs being pursued, promoted, or initiated.

Keeping financially solvent at any price is probably the lowest form of evangelism and yet it is one of the most frequently used! In actual fact, churches are doing the very thing they oppose in theory. They condemn our materialistic society for advocating "keeping up with the Joneses" and yet erect such elaborate buildings and pamper our every comfort until there is no money for missions and no time for outreach. The same members who are goaded from pulpits concerning their thirst for material things are requested and expected to support elaborate congregational buildings. In addition, "staff infection" is prevalent; that is, more paid personnel is on hand than a church can justify, and money is needed for its continuance. It is understandable that money may become the motive for outreach. At times, to the newcomer, the Church appears to stress but two requirements for membership. One is Confession of Faith in the Lord Jesus and the other is a willingness to support the

Church financially. All too often we stress the latter and completely ignore the former.

The Largest Church in Town

There are churches that take pride in the efforts of evangelism that enabled them to become the largest church in town. Church newspaper advertisements sometimes reveal Pharisaical pride in attendance. LARGEST SUNDAY SCHOOL IN TOWN blares forth from advertisements. Some churches will maintain this position even if it means running roughshod over all other churches and the united efforts of the other congregations in the community.

Prestige of Pastor and People

The evangelistic efforts of some congregations seem designed to maintain the prestige of the pastor and/or people. Their efforts to guide individuals to become persons in their own right and believers in Christ are conspicuously absent. Such churches sin against those drawn into such a situation. They lead not to the Master, but to masters, masters who would use and manipulate others instead of leading them by serving, masters who abuse the privileges of the Gospel.

It is wonderful to reach everyone for Christ and His Kingdom, but it behooves us to be careful as to the motives behind such efforts. The times demand our best and the Gospel is worthy of it.

Two

Craving for
the Creative

There are millions of Christians throughout the world who are deeply concerned about the present condition of the Church, and who want to do something. Theirs is a sincere willingness to sacrifice to bring an awakening in our midst.

The situation in many churches is not ideal, but of what value is a complaining spirit without alternate proposals that can be expected to work reasonably well and improve the Church's condition? If the Church is missing the mark, where is the target area at which the Church should be shooting? Constructive guidance must be given. Millions yearn for prophets, priests, pastors, and laity to lead them creatively to new birth.

As never before, the world needs leadership paced by commitment, constructive programs, and the example of excellence in spiritual service. Christian leadership is essential if the Church is to have a spiritual impact on today's world.

There is much that is still right with the Church. The same motives and methods that have been abused can be used creatively. There is abundant evidence to indicate that this will involve more than mere attendance at "religious" services. Some faithful attenders may be bigoted toward their fellowmen and calloused toward society's needs. Their spiritually superior attitude is one which Christ Himself cannot remove.

Life is too short to neglect accomplishing all that we can. We are not called to be merely good, but to be the best. We are not called to be busy, but to be *believers*, committed completely to Christ. We are not called simply to plan, but also to pray and to praise.

Genuine Fellowship

Creative concern is not present in most church programs. Congregational fellowship falls far short of the standards of our Saviour. It is not gained through a social get-together with a glad slap on the back by all for all. Fellowship is a deep awareness that we belong to one another and to the Lord Jesus Christ. It involves prayer, sacraments, study of the Word, and honesty with the self and with others. It is an experience, not a form of conduct.

What are some positive thoughts that can contribute to the aliveness of the Church today? What needs to be stressed to meet the demands of modern times? How can concern be made incarnate in meaningful outreach of evangelism and personal relationships?

Christian personal concern involves the realization that evangelism is not simply a pragmatic or utilitarian function of the Church. It is the design, principle, and teaching that God sent His Son into the world. This was concern at its highest and best. If Christ had waited until everyone on earth pleaded for a Redeemer, He never would have come. Concern cannot wait until the world in a unified voice cries, "This is what we want." It must spring from the Divine imperative within the hearts of believers, from a drive that will not let them do less than attempt to reach others. The world is the object of Christian love, not the energizing force. Our motivating force is God who lives within us and compels us to go forth. The world is the recipient of His love through us, not the revealer of it. Within the framework of the fellowship of His Church, God has chosen to reveal Himself.

With Believers at Least Once a Week

Basic to any new insight for the Institutional Church is the fact that believers should meet with other believers at least once a week. This is necessary to remain spiritually "sharp." The Holy Spirit speaks through others; our being with others is of great benefit both to us and to them.

It is amazing how we have come to reverence a certain day and time for our corporate worship. Sunday morning attendance for a particular hour of worship *is* the Church to most people. Pastors and people are both guilty of conveying this false concept and doctrine.

The early Church could not meet at a regular hour every Sunday, so they met on any day and at any time when meeting was possible. Sometimes they met in the wee hours of the morning and were home before daybreak. Persecution drove them to this. Yet, wise is the modern Church that maintains programs enabling believers to meet whenever possible for them to do so. This wise programing is a far cry from the "sacredness" attached to an 11:00 A.M. Sunday morning corporate worship service.

If you feel this special-day-and-time attitude toward fellowship does not prevail, ask individuals if they attended church this week. Many will excuse themselves with "Oh no, I had to work," or "I was ill and couldn't come," or "I was out of town," or "We had company." It has not dawned upon them that the Sunday service is not the Church.

It is almost impossible to get individuals to teach children during the Sunday morning worship hour. They are willing to support missionaries in the heart of Africa, but are not missionary-minded enough to miss a Sunday morning worship service in the cause of teaching. Yet, what a wonderful spiritual opportunity teaching religion is for the mature Christian who could very well meet at another service in the week for worship. Thousands of church members neglect worship each week for lesser reasons than the teaching of children.

The emphasis needed today should not be on how many we can get to attend one particular church service, but on how we can encourage every believer to meet with other believers at least once a week. Of course, many if not most people will still assemble on Sunday morning, but if work, illness, or other legitimate reasons prevent this attendance there should be other opportunities for corporate worship.

Why is Sunday morning so sacred? Sunday night, midweek service, youth meeting, or any other church activity can also provide undergirding in the faith. Mature leaders might forgo Sunday morning worship for those who are weaker in the faith. Those strong in the faith could serve as representatives for Christ for those reluctant to participate other than on Sunday morning.

There might be more good done by mature Christians calling in homes on Sunday morning than is done by their sitting week after week listening to sermons seeking to stimulate them to do what they have not been doing and do not intend to do. If they are mature in the faith, are they not in a position to go out and call at an hour when most Protestant people are at home? Some church members would be startled to have a loyal church person visit their home midmorning on Sunday. This timing probably would cause more of an impact than any other personal call that could be made.

This is not to reflect unduly on Sunday morning worship,

but it is an effort to remove it from the place of being more sacred than people. There is no sacred or secular time in God's sight. His promise is to be with those assembled in His name any time and anywhere.

We need to teach people that, if they are unable to attend Sunday morning worship, they should attend one of the other services or activities of the congregation during the week. As for the shut-in, believers should be invited to his home; a blessing is in store for them as well as for him, and it is spiritually enriching and encouraging to all involved.

There is no excuse for a believer to go week after week without meeting with other believers. This is a tragedy. And it is a reflection on what has been taught directly or indirectly when individuals or shut-ins say they have not been able to attend church for months or years. Through effort and example, leaders must demonstrate that the Church is God's people. A shut-in should have believers come to his home—to sing, to pray, to study the Word, and to share the glorious treasures of God. Tape-recorded services could be available for such gatherings.

Complete concern is manifest when no person is missed whom God has placed as a responsibility of a particular congregation. Not one shut-in, one ill person, one faithful attender, or one indifferent person should be neglected.

The Source of Concern

Deep concern leading to effective ministry comes from God. It is He who is constantly ministering to us and calling us to others. God ministers His love unto man through man. He is not restricted in mission to a specific congregation or a certain denomination. The Church is ministering to individuals whenever a person renders service in the name of Christ.

A sign of Christian maturity is the ability to appreciate and appropriate God's love from any and all sources. The Christian mailman, teacher, doctor, businessman, garbage collector, and so on are all used by God to express His love for us and to meet our needs. To say "no one from the Church has called on me for five years" is a glaring revelation of our misunderstanding of the Church.

The Church is more than a particular building on a particular corner with some of your particular acquaintances as its members. The Church is God's. It is comprised of men everywhere who name the name of Jesus. We know this in our minds, but we must accept it in our hearts. Essentially, a pastor is no more sacred than a ditch digger, a missionary no more spiritual than an office-machine operator. The crux of the matter is whether or not our life is dedicated to God and our talents are being used in whatever capacity He may be directing. In this light, it is obvious that we are constantly being ministered unto by Christ, who has expressed and who is expressing Himself through His Church.

Stress the Positive

There are positive thoughts which can create life in the Church *today*. They do not have to wait until the seventies to be verbalized or realized. All the present organizational structure of congregational life need not be changed. Our concern must become incarnate in thought and ultimately in action.

Personal concern, depth evangelism, meeting the world's needs, call it what you may, it cannot wait any longer. It must spring from the Divine imperative within the hearts of believers that will not let them do otherwise than to go to others.

Christ did not say, "Go ye into all the world," simply

23

because the world needed going into, but also because those who believe need others to maintain a vital relationship to Him. Evangelism is not something that exists because the world is lost, but because the believer is saved. It is the extension of God's love not necessarily because some are in darkness, but because there are those who "walk in the light."

Thus, concern is the result of an inner conviction, not an outward calling. It is an inward compulsion that propels the believer into action. Concern is not just a reaction to the evils which exist in the world; it is the very nature of God to love and to extend Himself. If we are created in His image by birth and rebirth, this same extending love is a part of us. Concern simply because of the needs of people will lead to despair, but concern because of the inner force of the Spirit will lead to dedication and faithfulness in the face of all obstacles.

New Perspectives

With the emphasis upon believers meeting with other believers at least once a week regardless of time or place, and that God ministers unto us through those who follow His Way, concern—evangelism—takes on a different perspective.

We are now at a point where individuals are ministered unto not merely to get them to attend meetings, but to meet whatever are the needs in their lives. Further, we function not only to meet the needs in the lives of others, but also to meet our own needs. Many of these needs were created the moment we believed.

Attendance, financial giving, the praise of men, prestige, and other inferior motives fade into the background when genuine concern is placed first. The Christian's service to Christ becomes more than encouraging individuals to attend Sunday morning worship and disparaging them when they

24

don't. (Service) becomes an attempt to convey that "one life is worth more than the whole world." Now we minister not to (manipulate,) but that all may see God. We earnestly want all to know "Our Father and their Father, our God and their God."

MOTIVATION

High

what God is
what has happened to us
— what we are,
+ are becoming

Meet people's need
— ea. worth
more than all planet
— not manipulation →

Low

attendance.
F en avied giving
Praise of Men
Prestige

manipulation
of people

Three

"Unto the Least
of These…"

[handwritten: At what point do most members meet persons within the range of our corporate and personal responsibility as members of the Body of X? need of personal canvass?]

Eliminate the efforts of the Every Member Canvass, the few contacts made with families who are not attending Sunday morning worship, and what have you left in the program of concern of most congregations? Too often, nothing!

The leadership in such congregations will acknowledge that it is best to meet a person at his point of need, but in practice do the opposite. An honest appraisal of congregational concern is always in order. In order to think more concretely concerning ministry to individuals, the following specific suggestions are made.

[handwritten: Be put in relationship with…]

THE GREAT DEED—KNOWING JESUS CHRIST

Christians should realize and admit that the greatest need of any individual is to know Jesus Christ. This answers the basic problem of life and gets to the root of many of the troubles and illnesses of the world. Knowing Him brings purpose to life. *[handwritten: Re-orientation of life]*

The direct statement that you need Jesus almost always means very little to an individual. He interprets this as an affront to his own goodness and self-reliance, preaching down to him, or an effort to convert him against his will.

In God's wisdom He so made man that he does not automatically submit to the words of others. What terrible shape the world would be in if we bowed down to every word uttered by our leaders, even our church leaders. God has ordained that men must see in deed, not just in words, if they are going to accept the teachings of another. This fact makes mandatory a life of personal concern on the part of Christians in efforts of depth evangelism. *the DEED*

It is more difficult to minister to people at depth than to make casual contacts for the Church, but it is much more rewarding. When we are striving not for involvement in a particular program or for attendance at a scheduled service, but simply to meet individuals where they are with what they need, this is Christian concern. The other is Church connivance.

It is strange to the modern mind that in the four Gospels there is no record of Christ's ever inviting anyone to attend the synagogue. It is not in the Gospels, but in the Epistles that we find, "Forsake not the assembling of yourselves . . ." (Heb. 10:25). Perhaps it was not necessary. Perhaps Christ took for granted the activities of the synagogue as He apparently did not put forth effort to invite others to a particular service, even though it was His custom to participate. He endeavored at every opportunity to teach, heal, and proclaim the Good News that God was reconciling the world unto Himself, yet he did not carry on a great attendance campaign for the synagogue. His ministry was so natural and constant that it has taken the insight of succeeding generations to appreciate that reconciliation was taking place through Him.

In a sense each of us is Christ to someone else. We are not divine. We are not perfect. We are *in Christ*, vessels that

How can we corporately + individually
1 Reach — units
2 Teach — The X Way
3 Heal — alienation, sin etc.
4 Proclaim — Reconciliation

can be used to lead another to Him. God was *in* Christ, not *through* Christ, reconciling the world unto Himself (II Cor. 5:19). Christ was more than a channel, He was the Son of God. We are more than channels. We are the children of God (I John 3:1).

Christians convey to others the God they serve. This is best done as we meet, confront, encounter others at their point of need. We do not seek individuals because of what they can do for the Church, but because of what God has done for us and can do for them. We can say with Paul of old, "I seek not yours, but you." (II Cor. 12:14). In deed as well as in word, we can say that we are interested in you even if you do not accept our interpretation of the Church and worship. Simply because of our great need as believers, we reach out to you. This is true evangelism, and this type of congregational ministry can be extended under many circumstances.

When One Moves

There are always many adjustments in moving to a new community, and there is a vacuum in the lives of those who have recently moved. It is a time when every member of a family is a challenge to the Church.

The husband is getting adjusted to a new job and new friends. Perhaps he has been promoted, but he faces the occupational hazards of his success. Or he may have been demoted, and he faces this humiliation.

The wife may have to find employment, or at least have to make new friends at PTA, clubs, church, and in the neighborhood. These are days of tension for her.

The children must adjust at school, and they too must endure the frustration of forsaking old friends and finding new ones.

The Church has a message for such families. Help must be extended with no strings attached: "If you come to our parish, we will help you."

Illness

Nothing causes a family to realize the frailty of life more than serious illness. And there is no family that goes many years without an immediate member, a relative, or a close friend being afflicted. The need of faith comes into sharper focus during serious illness and there is a great desire for that which is beyond human resources.

Christians must realize that not only is one member ill, but that the entire family is upset. Frequently, there is some effort to minister to the one who is in the hospital, but forgotten are the other members of the family. All too often they know more about the patient's condition than he does, and they are more inwardly troubled. During extreme illness a patient under heavy sedation suffers little pain and certainly far less anguish of heart and soul than do his loved ones. It takes much effort, but it is richly rewarding for the Church to minister to all during illness.

Death

We are never ready to give up a loved one. We never arrive at the point where we can say, "Now the last breath can be taken." Even when suffering is so great that we realize it is wrong to pray for life to be prolonged, it is difficult for us to accept death. Death, whether it comes suddenly or follows a long illness, always brings the same results. There is the finality of separation, the burdens of sorrow, despair, grief, unfulfilled desires, and a multitude of other problems. The loved ones who remain need and desire the undergirding of the Church as never before. The resurrection message of hope in Christ becomes real when there is new life seen through the ministering of the member of the Church to the bereaved. They cannot hear the words of the funeral service as loudly and clearly as they can the deeds of the faithful. The funeral message converts very few, but a response of love on the part of Christians reaches many.

Loss of Job

Losing one's job can create a crisis in any home. The loss may be the result of physical disability, the closing of a plant, automation, or any one of many factors. Whatever the reason, the net result is discouragement and ultimate despair if another job is not forthcoming.

We may have heard or read about people who love to sit back and collect their unemployment check, but the vast majority want work that brings dignity and a decent living to them. Sometimes they cannot find a job that they are capable of doing. The Church is not, and it cannot be, an employment agency. Yet, it can certainly lend a sympathetic ear to the unemployed. It is not asking too much to have Christians spend time in specific prayer for specific individuals who are unemployed. This prayer should not be made without willingness to put feet to the prayer.

It is sad, but often true, that if one does not support the Church financially he is not the recipient of the ministry of the congregation. It is not right for an unemployed person to be made to feel self-conscious about participating in the life of the Church simply because he cannot contribute.

Marriage

"We want to help you establish and maintain a Christian home," should be what the newlyweds hear the Church saying and see it doing. Our homes should serve as examples and our guidance be given with this in mind. Marriage ministry should not end with the wedding ceremony. Counseling sessions before and after marriage serve a purpose, but they are only part of the answer. Opportunity should always exist for help in a marriage. This takes much effort and it cannot be done through mass meetings or by one set pattern. The blood, sweat, and tears of Christians at the proper time and in the proper way would prevent many modern marital disasters. The homes of families in the parish should serve as examples of marriage stability.

Baptism

One way that individuals reveal their religious concern is by requesting Christian baptism for themselves and their children. They may not know or understand all the doctrinal positions, governmental structures, or particulars of programing in their local church; but they want their children baptized into the Christian faith. Orchids to a church that does not question such a request even by the most inactive, but uses it as a time in which to minister. The parents can be pointed to the Pioneer of our faith. The children should not be denied this sacred rite. In churches where infant baptism is not practiced, the request will come when children are older, but the response by the Church should still be such as to meet this need. Meeting the need is more than just administering a sacrament; it is imparting the reason for it and having all experience the warmth of Christian fellowship.

Divorce

Many marriages fail and many others are constantly on the verge of failure. The death of a spouse is a trying experience, but in many cases divorce is more so. Many divorced individuals say that they would have chosen a long period of physical illness, perhaps even death, rather than a broken home. Divorce is more frightening and reflects more upon an individual as far as society is concerned.

The Church has too often and for too long sat back when distressing situations have arisen in a parish. Although the Church cannot look with favor on divorce, it must take positive steps to help the parties concerned. The Church does not expel the divorced from membership, but it must be more than tolerant. It must be tactful and helpful; it must avoid the cruel attitude often evident in the past toward people in this awkward position; it must face the many problems of divorce, and not simply by trying to get the troubled to attend services. Regardless of the family's reactions to the institution and their responses to its program, Christians should be there to help. Such troubled souls need the undergirding of the faithful.

It is amazing how Jesus Christ undergirded even those whom society labeled as extremely immoral. He did not say they should be immoral, but at the same time He did not withhold Himself from them. He did not stoop to what they were doing, but neither did He walk away from them. Every member of the family involved in a divorce is a mission field ripe unto harvest. Not only the ones who come to the pastor of their own volition, but each person in the divorced family needs TLC (tender loving care). Children suffer much in divorce. Also, the one who often appears most guilty of bringing about the shameful situation is frequently most in

need and at least subconsciously is longing for an understanding heart and hand.

How often have you heard, "I didn't want a divorce and
I felt it would never happen to me." This is an open
invitation to someone to listen and to minister. It should
come through as loud and clear as the more "spiritual"
question, "Lord, what wouldst thou have me to do?" How
sensitive are we as believers when words of concern are uttered in our presence?

Visitors at Church Services

Spiritual searching is often revealed through attendance at
worship service. The highest motives may not always be
uppermost in a person's mind when he visits a church, but he
may be saying, "Can anyone help me?" The believer should
be spiritually sensitive; he cannot wait until the "seeking"
verbalize their desires.

It is difficult to speak about the deep feelings of the soul.
It is almost impossible to articulate why we attend church
even if we have done so for years. This spiritual searching
can take various forms: group study, serving others, or sharing in depth conversations. Such things in and by themselves
are neither perfection nor the way of salvation, but are
indicative of a person's desiring something more out of life.
These cries from the deep should be heard and heeded by
sensible and sensitive believers.

Moral Defeat

A family is so often open to the comfort and encouragement of others when one of its members has experienced
moral failure. Perhaps a son has run off and married a girl

unacceptable to his parents. Or a daughter has found herself with child, and the father is completely objectionable to her family. The husband may be unfaithful, or the wife, or both. Such incidents happen every day in thousands of homes throughout our land and are open opportunities for Christian concern.

Moral problems must be seen in the light of Christ's purpose. He came to the world not so much because the world was lost, but because of who He is. He could not do otherwise. His very nature would not let Him remain outside the world. His very nature made it absolutely necessary that He come, and not just because we cannot save ourselves. He could not say "no" to the world, not only because thousands cried out for deliverance, but also because He could not be true to His nature and stay away.

We do not necessarily go to others because they are lost or in danger of being lost, but because believers are saved and are in the process of being saved. It is God who passes judgment upon individuals. Our chief concern should be that we be faithful to Him. Therefore, we go to others to listen, to love, and to lend a helping hand.

In the Armed Services

If ever the Church had an opportunity to express love and concern it is to those in military service or committed to other worthy causes away from their home community.

Today, there is hardly a family in our nation that does not have one of its members or a close friend or relative in the armed services. It is never a pleasant experience to send a son away to the Army. Even if there is no open war there are still the physical, spiritual, and moral dangers to which he will be exposed. Temptations are intensified when one is thousands of miles from home and loved ones. Moral resistance is lowered when one is beset by homesickness and the influence of others who are lonely. If ever the Church had an open field to minister, it is to these individuals. We should seek to minister not only to the one away in service, but also to his family at home—to his parents, or his wife and children, who all need the strength of the Church.

No church should ever be guilty of saying, "Well, he never came when he had the opportunity, so why should we write and keep contact while he is in service?" Neither in word nor in action should it say, "The family is inactive. Why go out of our way for their son?" This is gross sin and worthy of God's wrath.

Today there are homes that are saddened beyond words with the news that their sons will never come home. A brief memorial service weeks later can never replace their loss. The mother, father, brother, sister will never be the same. Comfort and solace must come from the Church not for just an hour, but for the days and years ahead.

Shut-Ins

Shut-ins are not necessarily old people, but any who are unable to carry on normal activity. Most churches have a very inadequate ministry to them. Shut-ins may or may not be outgoing, pleasant to visit, or those once active in church. But a church interested only in those who can come to public services and swell attendance and finances will never do a very effective job.

The soul of a person flat on his back for months is as important in the sight of God as the tither sitting in the pew every Sunday. We will be held as accountable for the aged widow neglected in her lonely hours as for the many healthy ones who have been unfaithful and unwarned by us. Upon our consciences will be those souls who could not participate in public worship because of illness, and whom we failed to confront with commitment to Christ. We must see that all to whom God has given us the privilege to minister receive the ministry of believers. We are called not to a few, but to every one in our outreach.

Areas Too Numerous to Mention

There are many other areas that we could mention—the poor; the underprivileged; the handicapped; the retarded; the victims of modern technology, modern highways, urban renewal; and so on.

Interest in individuals is not hit-or-miss evangelism, but the programed personal concern that should be characteristic of every local congregation. It takes much work and careful planning, but it is the most helpful and spiritually rewarding to all.

Programed Concern (under Service in church)

CONCERNING PERSONAL CONCERN

Superficial evangelism is a little social activity mingled with deluded spiritual concepts. Personal concern is getting out of the bleachers and onto the playing field. There is a tremendous difference. Depth evangelism will and must involve individuals ready to take the bruising punishments of being actively in the contest. Such individuals are well aware that there is an adversary determined to prevent them from attaining the goal of meeting the needs of others, but they are equally aware of God's assurance to be ever with them. The personally concerned will train and discipline themselves, in order to participate in such a way that the Christian life will be shown in their every action. Theirs is more than a weekly or monthly night for calling on families; theirs is *Life* in the Spirit at all times.

Personal concern is a call to leaders who are willing to be bored, willing to take on tedious tasks, willing to go that second mile so that another may move one spiritual inch. Personal concern is a call . . . to those who are committed for commitment's sake to have no other aim in life than to glorify God, to those who do not keep both eyes firmly fixed on the attendance or financial sheet, to those who in spite of obstacles believe they will overcome, to those who do not count faithfulness by what is so often termed success, to those who realize it is not how active one is in the machinery of the institution but how faithful one is to Jesus Christ, to those who are willing to lift up Christ not so much by *doing* as by *being*.

Deep personal concern is a challenge to go forth willing to serve without being served, to give without expecting to receive, to understand without always lamenting being misunderstood, to help when help is not received gratefully, to trust when all seems in vain, to pray when it would be easier to complain, to have a reason for faith and positive action when it would be much easier to find excuses not to get involved, and to say with confidence and conviction, "This is the way and I am going to walk in it."

The succeeding pages present ideas about ministering to all. A program serves a worthy purpose if it remains our slave and does not become our master. The Church ministers wherever believers are. It is our task to see that this ministry is the most effective possible. The framework of a local parish program is not sacred per se. The sacredness comes from our understanding of what we should be doing and then having the courage to do it. We are called to Be in Christ. How this manifests itself must always be scrutinized very carefully by each believer.

Hosea 6:6, as translated in *Living Prophecies*, has a word for our day: "I don't want your sacrifices—I want your love; I don't want your offering—I want you to know me."

Four

Person to
Person

Thousands of church members are indifferent to their responsibilities in the Kingdom and thousands of leaders in the Church are indifferent to these members. Communication, between those who are active and those who once were and could again be, is urgently needed. This will not come naturally or be maintained automatically. If accomplished at all, it will be through the efforts of those who are committed to Christ and realize that their needs are met most adequately when they are working to His glory, by those who have the unique talent of being able to finish what they start.

A local congregation is not simply a mass of people. Individuals should not be lost in bigness of membership and complexity of organization. The congregation should be a living organism. It should have a heart and a vibrant personality.

Some people delude themselves by thinking that if they ignore the problems of administration, their church will be more personal, and individuals will not become mere numbers in the congregation. The opposite is true, however. If administration is neglected, many become not even numbers; they are completely neglected.

Church administration consumes the bulk of the pastor's and church leaders' time. Yet, the feeling persists that administration is sinful and that only prayer meeting, corporate worship, and the like are sacred.

Pastors, lay leaders, and denominational officials must come to a greater appreciation of the fact that statistics are as sacred as sermons, facts as necessary as faith, and that all things are sacred in their proper perspective. A congregation that ministers to all must regard even its record-keeping as a sacred ministry.

Why Lack of Concern?

Some of the reasons for a lack of systematic personal concern for every individual in the congregation are as follows:

1. It is hard work to minister systematically and seriously to people as individuals.

2. All too often pastors are not particularly talented at, or enthused about, administration.

3. Many lay people, as well as pastors, believe that administration, regardless of how it may be done or directed, is not spiritual.

4. Perhaps the greatest reason for administrative neglect is a lack of guidance and effective tools to do the job.

Positive Steps

No one in the congregation should receive undue attention, yet no one should be neglected. In most cases, neglect stems from the lack of a systematic approach to the problem of personally ministering to each and every individual.

Securing and creatively using information is a tremendously time-consuming, tedious, and often thankless task. Yet, in any business or profession, it is essential. Concern cannot be divorced from practical application. It is a sin to speak of the Church's shortcomings and offer no positive alternatives or solutions. For too long emphasis upon personal commitment and administrative efficiency has been with words only; guidance for implementing the words has been lacking.

It is because of this that I have through the years given much thought to the development of administrative tools for the local congregation. I have tried to use tools that are effective, efficient, and economical. My aim is to help Christians *do* adequately what the Church teaches should be done. These tools have been incorporated into what is known as the Systematic Ministry Program.

The Pastor

The pastor must set the pace of personal concern; he must make the congregation aware of the potential and power of personal concern. The congregation can rise no higher than the leadership the pastor gives and the spirit in which he pioneers, projects, and propels concern and creativity.

The creative use of the proper tools will awaken a congregation to new visions of vital personal ministry to members and prospective members, Church education, evangelism, worship, stewardship, youth work, and the like. It is wise indeed to invest a few dollars on materials to minister personally and effectively to those for whom a building costing many thousands of dollars was built.

Willing Workers

Experience has shown that, given the proper tools, volunteer help will more than adequately care for the extra manpower that is needed for an effective personal ministry. Most congregations have a larger percentage of their membership skilled in the areas of typing and office work than in teaching. Yet, congregations constantly seek volunteer teachers and overlook the value of involvement in office work. Congregations with employed office staff will find that the time-saving factor alone makes efficient tools a wise investment, even with inexperienced volunteers. Those employed get more done in less time, and every minute saved, every penny saved, is good and essential stewardship.

The forms described in the following section present possible solutions to the complexities of administration and personal concern.

1. Family Record Form

The Family Record form is used to record information concerning the entire family. Space is provided for name, date of birth, baptism, church membership, and confirmation date of every family member. Also, there is room for the wedding anniversary date, hobbies, family code, address, phone number, and general comments.

Multiple copies can be made through the use of carbon paper. The original can be kept in the office file and copies distributed to those who have need of them. Copies should be funneled to the departments throughout the church where names of members of the family may be useful. For example, when the teacher of the third grade is given Johnny Smith's name, he can receive information concerning the whole Smith family. He can thus minister more adequately to this

FAMILY RECORD

FAMILY NAME		ADDRESS		PHONE		CODE
WEDDING ANNIVERSARY	HUSBAND'S OCCUPATION		WIFE'S OCCUPATION		DATE INFORMATION RECORDED	

A	FIRST NAMES	BIRTH			BAPTISM			CONFIRMED			JOINED CHURCH			COMMENTS
		MO.	DAY	YR.	MO.	DAY	YR.	MO.	DAY	YR.	MO.	DAY	YR.	
	H.													
	W.													
	1.													
	2.													
	3.													
	4.													
	5.													
	6.													

A – a mark in this column designates the individual for whom this particular copy of the form was given to you.

Family Record

pupil, because he knows what members of the family are baptized, are members of the congregation, and so forth. Little Johnny is now more than just a name to his teacher.

Some churches show only the month and day for the wedding anniversary and adult birthdays on all copies, but the office file copy usually lists year dates as well.

A copy of family information for each member of their particular group should be available to choir directors, teachers of church school classes, age group directors, women's groups, Scouts, evangelism committee, and any other group in which individuals participate. When a copy of the form is given out, a checkmark in Column A designates for what member of the family it is intended. The Family Record also serves a worthy purpose when it comes to prospective and inactive members of a church, church school, or a church organization. The Family Record gets families better acquainted with one another, an essential in large congregations.

Family information should be kept current. When there is a birth, death, change of address, marriage, joining church, baptism, and so on, it should be entered on the form's office copy; where necessary, a corrected form should be prepared and made available to all needing the amended information.

To secure complete information about a family, some congregations may want to list the data they now have and mail this partially completed form to each family, requesting the form's completion and return to the church office. Smaller congregations may phone their members, using the form as a guide to secure the necessary information.

The pastor can help to develop and maintain current and accurate church files by securing information about the family on the occasions of his ministry to families: at the time of marriage, at baptisms, at reception of new members, and so on. The large majority of families appreciate the fact that the congregation is interested in them, and the use of a neat and adequate form adds dignity to the pastor's request for family information.

The following example shows the Family Record form in action:

Mr. and Mrs. John Doe and children, Mary and Jack, are formally transferring to a church they have been attending. The pastor secures from them the information necessary to complete the Family Record form. The original of the form is kept in the office file and carbon copies are made for those individuals who should know about the Doe family. The adult choir director receives a copy because Mr. Doe desires to sing in the choir; others receiving copies are the director of the adult church school class for couples, Mary's third-grade teacher, Jack's seventh-grade teacher, the Scoutmaster, and the youth fellowship adviser.

In other words, wherever any member of the family participates in the life of the congregation, the responsible person in that area receives a copy of the Family Record form with the pertinent information concerning the family.

2. Family Record Portfolio

The Family Record portfolio is a convenient holder for Family Record forms kept by various departments. It is made of heavy card stock and has four pockets on the inner right side providing room for records of (1) active members, (2) inactive members, and (3) prospective members and (4) for extra Family Record forms. The inner left side has a compartment in which the teacher, director, etc. can keep material pertinent to his class or organization.

A portfolio for Family Record forms should be made

LAST NAME _____   ADDRESS _____   PHONE _____   FAMILY CODE _____   PARISH ZONE _____

H. _____

W. _____

OCCUPATION

DATE INFO FIRST FILED

WEDDING ANNIVERSARY

	19	19	19	19	19	19	19	19	19	19	19	19	19	19	19	19
Yearly Fund 1																
Adult Fund 2																
Contribution Fund 3																

LOCAL CHURCH PARTICIPATION AND TOTAL ANNUAL
SUNDAY MORNING WORSHIP AND COMMUNION ATTENDANCE

FIRST NAME	Birth			Baptism			Confirmed			Membership																		
	M	D	Yr.	M	D	Yr.	M	D	Yr.	M	D	Yr.	19	19	19	19	19	19	19	19	19	19	19	19	19	19	19	19
H.																												
W.																												
1.																												
2.																												
3.																												
4.																												
5.																												
6.																												

Family Folder

available to all church school teachers, Scout leaders, ladies' circle leaders, youth fellowship leaders and advisers, committee chairmen and secretaries, and all other individuals who are using Family Record forms.

3. Family File Folder

This letter-sized file folder provides a place for the recording of information concerning each family of the congregation.

Printed on each folder is a place to record the following: name, address, phone, wedding anniversary, occupation of parents, parish zone, family code, total adult contributions for eighteen consecutive years, contacts with the family or an individual of the family made by a member of the staff or volunteer help, number of times each member of the family attended worship and/or Holy Communion annually for fourteen consecutive years, and each individual's activities in the parish. Also, there is plenty of room for comments to be written on the folder if desired.

Carbon copies of letters sent to any member of the family, comments concerning counseling situations, and other material can be filed in the Family File. If the family transfers to another church, the Family File folder can be forwarded with the letter of transfer. This is helpful to the leaders of the new congregation as the family assumes the responsibility of their new membership.

4. Registration Forms
for Worship Participation

Recording attendance is necessary if a congregation is to minister effectively to its members and to those who look to the Church for guidance. The use of the Registration Pad

Please register and pass the pad to the one next to you. When the pad is returned, notice the names of those seated with you and following the service get acquainted with one another.

WELCOMES

THIS CHURCH -- **YOU**

Name _____ Phone _____

Address_____
STREET, CITY, STATE, ZIP CODE
_____Member _____ Visitor _____First Time Here _____Desire a Call

Name _____ Phone _____

Address_____
STREET, CITY, STATE, ZIP CODE
_____Member _____ Visitor _____First Time Here _____Desire a Call

Name _____ Phone _____

Address_____
STREET, CITY, STATE, ZIP CODE
_____Member _____ Visitor _____First Time Here _____Desire a Call

Name _____ Phone _____

Address_____
STREET, CITY, STATE, ZIP CODE
_____Member _____ Visitor _____First Time Here _____Desire a Call

Name _____ Phone _____

Address_____
STREET, CITY, STATE, ZIP CODE
_____Member _____ Visitor _____First Time Here _____Desire a Call

Name _____ Phone _____

Address_____
STREET, CITY, STATE, ZIP CODE
_____Member _____ Visitor _____First Time Here _____Desire a Call

Name _____ Phone _____

Address_____
STREET, CITY, STATE, ZIP CODE
_____Member _____ Visitor _____First Time Here _____Desire a Call

Registration Pad

is the most efficient method of taking registration. It has a distinct advantage over the Pew Card method in having a much larger percentage of those present register at each service. Many attenders will not go to the bother of securing a card from the pew rack and filling in the requested information, but there is close to 100 per cent registration with the use of a pad that each person signs and passes to the next one in the pew.

There should be a Registration Pad provided for each pew so that all may register quickly. Also, if the pad is passed back to the end of the pew from which it started, each person can note who is seated in the pew with him and at the close of the service get acquainted with any strangers who may be present.

Each section of the Registration Pad has space for name, complete address, phone number, and a place to check if the registrant is a visitor, a member of the church, present for the first time, or if a call by the pastor or someone from the congregation is desired.

Each page of the Registration Pad is perforated into seven sections; by simply tearing the sheet apart at the points of perforation, the names of those present can quickly be alphabetized for recording in the attendance book. The perforated pad gives the flexibility of a card while securing a much greater degree of accuracy of registration.

In some congregations young people, junior ushers or usherettes, distribute the pads and pencils at an appropriate time in the service. This is an opportunity for youth involvement and also assures that there is a pad in every pew. Having the pads distributed overcomes the reluctance of anyone in a partially filled pew to retrieve a pad at the opposite end of the pew, or the stubbornness of one who refuses to use the pad or give others an opportunity to do so.

Registration of participants can be a meaningful part of

any service, whether pads are distributed or simply available in the pews. Experience has shown that very few individuals react negatively to registration. In fact, the large majority appreciate the concern shown and the tangible opportunity to witness their faithfulness in worship. Not only do those not faithful in attendance appreciate knowing they have been missed, but also registration helps them to realize that the congregation is taking corporate worship seriously.

If desired, Registration Pads can be printed in different colors to signify attendance at worship and at church school.

5. Attendance and Adult Contribution Form

The Attendance and Contribution form enables a congregation regularly to report not only finances but also attendance at worship and/or church school and at Holy Communion.

Space is available to mark weekly attendance and the total number of times present each quarter and annually for each member of the family. Also, this form records adult contributions and special offerings at Easter, Thanksgiving, Christmas, and other occasions.

Since NCR paper is used, one entry suffices for all copies. The address is entered only once and arranged for use with window envelopes. Forms are available for single, double, and triple fund envelopes and for quarterly or semi-annually reporting to each contributor.

A word should be said about the recording of attendance as well as contributions. Many congregations are accused of being concerned only about money and reporting nothing but contributions. Attendance is by far the more important aspect. A form covering both reports helps families to realize that their participation with other believers is just as important to a church as their contribution. For families where only children attend church services, the form calls the adults' attention to the need for contributions; for families who give but never attend, the report speaks of attendance.

A church's calling committee, finance committee, and nominating committee, among others, need this form. It can honestly be said that this type of record must be used before a church can appreciate how valuable it can be.

There is room on the form for quarterly, semi-annual, or annual personal comments by the pastor or chairman of the committee in charge of this information. The comment may express appreciation for the faithfulness of a family or some member of the family. It may simply mention that the family has been missed in worship services, or call attention to some special recognition a member of the family has received. The more personal the report, the greater the response to its use.

The pastor can use his dictating machine for making comments, and the secretary can record them on the Attendance and Contribution form. Using the family coding, a brief comment to each family will not take much of a pastor's time, but it is most encouraging to the families of the congregation.

For example, a pastor would put on his dictating machine: "S–16. We were happy to receive Dale and Sue as members on Palm Sunday." The secretary knows that the John Smith family is coded S–16 and simply types this comment on their form.

6. Personal Concern Form

The Personal Concern form is designed to give guidance and supply information concerning contacts with families and individuals and to implement further congregational ministry.

Personal Concern

"In as much as you have done it to the least of these, ye have done it unto me." Matt. 25:40

_____
            name   address   phone   family code

Will you please pray for and _____phone_____visit_____send letter_____send card to the above:

The following information given _____ may be helpful to you:
                                mo.   day   yr.

TO:

                                                              signed:_____

I followed through the above suggestions_____ and feel the following remarks will be of future value.
                                        mo.   day   yr.

FROM:

                                                              signed:_____

(Please keep the original copy. Return the second copy.)

_____

Personal Concern

This form, 8½" × 7", provides an original and two copies. Space is provided for the date and the name, address, and phone of the family to be contacted, pertinent information concerning the family for the person who is calling, and the name and address of the person making the contact. Emphasis is put upon prayer; the contact person is encouraged to phone, visit, or send a letter or card as the circumstances may warrant. There is space for the contact person to write comments. The address of the contact person and the church's address are placed for use with window envelopes.

The three copies serve the following purposes. One remains in the office file and provides a permanent record of the assignment. The other two are given or mailed to the contact person. After the contact, he is to write his comments and return one copy to the office file and keep one copy for himself.

7. Spiritual Prescription Form

Often the pastor's counseling leads him to suggest some tangible guidelines to the person being counseled. In most cases, these suggestions are given verbally and the individual is expected to remember and follow through to the best of his ability. The Spiritual Prescription form provides a neat and dignified way of giving specific guidance. It is spiritually oriented and blends dignity, efficiency, and uniformity with the counseling ministry.

The actual suggestion recorded here may be to read a particular book, to start to attend certain church services, to join a church group or organization, to see another professional person for related help, and so forth. Such suggestions are often too valuable to say at random and risk their being forgotten or misunderstood.

There is room on this letter-sized form for the name and

address of the one seeking help, the suggested date and time of the next counseling period, and comments by the counselor. The church's or counselor's name and address and phone can also be imprinted.

There are two copies to the Spiritual Prescription form. One copy is kept by the counselor and the other given or mailed to the one being counseled. Addressing is designed for use with window envelopes. The copy sent to the person being counseled has space for comments, thoughts, or questions that may arise and that he may wish to consider with the counselor at their next meeting.

The counselor's copy can be placed in the person's permanent file, and there is room to make comments concerning the interview if desired. The use of the Spiritual Prescription form increases the pastor's effectiveness, and individuals appreciate the form as a tangible show of concern. In addition, complete and accurate records eliminate the shortcomings of memory regarding counseling situations.

8. Church-o-Gram

The Church-o-Gram provides a distinctively "Church" tone to a rapid and efficient method of communication. It adds dignity to the speed-letter concept.

Secretarial help is expensive, but prompt replies to letters are desirable. The three-part Church-o-Gram can help solve this problem. Messages can be written or typed. One part of the form is retained by the sender and two are sent to the recipient. He, in turn, types his reply, keeping the original and returning the carbon copy. There is always a record of what was written by the sender, as well as what was received and returned.

The inside address, which can be imprinted, and the re-

"Come unto me all ye that labor and are heavy laden and I will give Thee rest." Mt. 11:28

spiritual prescription

Please give prayerful consideration to the following:

FROM THE OFFICE OF:

DATE ___ / / ___

•

DATE OF
NEXT APPOINTMENT ___ / / ___

SIGNED _____

•

LIST ABOVE ANY QUESTIONS, COMMENTS, THOUGHTS YOU MAY WANT TO CONSIDER FURTHER.

Spiritual Prescription

church-o-gram

TO •

**M
E
S
S
A
G
E**

SIGNED _____

**R
E
P
L
Y**

FROM •

SIGNED _____

_____ / / _____
DATE

SENDER RETAIN SECOND SHEET — RECIPIENT RETAIN FIRST SHEET — RETURN THIRD TO SENDER.

DETACH FOR FOLLOW-UP

Church-o-Gram

turn address are arranged for use with a #10 window envelope.

The pastor, organizations within the local congregation, denominational and interdenominational leaders and officials, and so on will find the Church-o-Gram easy to use, efficient, and economical. Its cost is less than that of letterhead stationery, carbon paper, and second sheets, to say nothing of time a secretary must take to put these ingredients together.

9. Responsibility Form

The Responsibility form provides for efficient contacting of members and friends of the congregation. It may be used to determine reservations for a banquet, to notify people of a choir party or a special congregational meeting, in the enlistment of new members, or for any other purpose for which a number of people need to be contacted.

There is space to mark the date the list is prepared, the purpose of the list, to whom it is given, the date it is returned, and the response of those contacted. A carbon copy of the list should be made available to the general chairman of the event so that he has a record of who is responsible for contacting whom. The individual making the contact returns his sheet with a comment concerning each call.

This form can also serve to list all the individuals of a particular class, age group, organization, or year of birth, shut-ins, and so on within the congregation. The form is prepunched for a two- or three-ring notebook.

10. For-Get-Me-Not Form

Efficiency in administration demands specific and clear guidance to those responsible for tasks being accomplished, and the "For-Get-Me-Not" form serves this purpose. There is space on this $8\frac{1}{2}'' \times 7''$ form to write the name of the person delegating, and the name of the person receiving, the assignment. Two copies are given to the one responsible for following through on suggestions, and one copy is retained by the office or by the person delegating the assignment. Comments are made on the two copies concerning the completion of the assignment, and one copy is returned to the office and the other kept by the person fulfilling the task. If mailed, window envelopes can be used for sending and returning the form without refolding it.

The use of these forms proves helpful to pastors, church school teachers, elders, sextons, women's organizations, or any other group involved in assigning tasks to others. They are especially helpful to the pastor in making suggestions for committee consideration. It is relatively easy for the secretary or chairman of the committee to jot down comments as to what took place at a committee meeting and to see that the pastor gets a copy of this information immediately.

11. Worship Service Information

Whether worship services are planned weeks in advance or information is gathered weekly, the Worship Service Information form is helpful. It has a place to list date of the service, hymns, ushers, prelude, offertory, postlude, special music, sermon title, Scripture, anthems, responsive reading, and so on.

Carbon copies of this information can be made available for the pastor, organist, music director, and the individual who prepares the bulletin. The forms are prepunched for filing in a two- or three-ring notebook.

Also available is a sheet for recording the dates on which certain hymns are used. This form is numbered 1 through 600 and has room to write the date of the use of each hymn number. The dates of the period covered by the sheet can be written at the top of the form. Such guidance permits better and more varied use of the hymnbook.

12. The Christian Funeral Form

Many people believe the Church should give guidance to families prior to the shock of the death of a loved one. The Christian Funeral form provides this guidance. It enables a family to take a comprehensive look at some of the things that should be considered carefully by every individual concerning death. Having such a form as a guide is appreciated by families and it enables the Church to assume another of the proper roles in its ministry.

There is space for designating whether an individual desires a traditional or a memorial service; where he wishes the service to be conducted; what choices he may have as to a funeral director, flowers, gifts to the Church or favorite charity, pallbearers, music, favorite poetry, Scripture; whether or not he desires to donate his eyes to the eye bank, body to medical school; whether or not he has left a will.

An individual should fill out several copies of this form. One copy should be retained by him, and the other copies given to his church, funeral director, attorney, and a close friend. This helps assure that one's wishes concerning one's funeral arrangements will be followed.

The forms are so economically priced that a special mailing of a copy to every family of the parish can be done reasonably, or a copy can be inserted into a mailing of the parish letter. Extra copies should always be available at the church office.

The use of these forms encourages more families to remember the Church in their wills, present memorial gifts to the Church, and contribute to the Church or their favorite charity at the time of the death of a loved one.

13. In Loving Memory Cards

Frequently at the time of a funeral many flowers are given, but in the long weeks and months following the bereaved are practically forgotten by friends. The Church must give guidance for a continued ministry to those who sorrow. The In Loving Memory card helps in this ministry. The card should be given or mailed to the bereaved during the immediate days of bereavement. Arrangements with a florist should be made by the giver to have flowers delivered at a future date. The suggested date may be a month later, several months later, perhaps on the bereaved's birthday, or at some other special time. There are often flowers put on the altar in church in observance of a special day or event in the life of an individual. Some will find this ministry enhanced through sending flowers of remembrance to the home of a friend. Sometimes flowers can say what words can never convey.

The In Loving Memory card reads as follows:

IN LOVING MEMORY
OF

_____

flowers will be received by you

_____

month, day, year

FROM

name _____

address_____

The following poem appears on the card:

Men's gardens fair adorn the land
With fragrance sweet and beauty grand,
From lowly seed appears the green,
Which forms a part of earth's fleeting scene.

Thus our body is the seed,
Which serves a vital short lived need,
But the soul of man, the eternal flower,
Is nurtured forever by God's power.

14. The Wedding Form

The form entitled "Your Wedding" provides for the recording of many wedding details: the name of the bride and groom; the other members of the wedding party and their part in the wedding; when and where the ceremony was conducted; the organist and soloist; the place and time of the reception; the dates of counseling with the pastor; suggested resource reading; the specific rules of the local church, and many other pertinent facts.

The form lends dignity to the securing of the necessary information and helps the couple feel that the Church is sincerely concerned about their wedding and that nothing is left to chance.

Every couple planning to marry should be provided with at least two copies of the form; more copies should be available if many people must have wedding information. The form serves as a guide to them as they collect all the necessary information and see that in due time the pastor, organist, soloist, and others of the wedding party receive the required data.

A copy of this inexpensive form mailed to every family

in the congregation would indirectly as well as directly give much guidance in the area of the Christian wedding.

15. Minutes of Meetings

The Minutes of Meetings form provides for a uniform and neat recording of minutes. For each meeting, space is provided for date, place, time of beginning and end, presiding chairman, secretary, those present, and record of business considered.

Several copies of a committee's minutes can be had on these forms for less than the cost of a stencil. Carbon copies can be made for the pastor, chairman, secretary, and any others to whom the minutes would be useful.

An advantage of this form is that volunteer secretaries of committees can type copies at home and not bother with a mimeograph machine or consume a church secretary's time. Yet, all minutes will appear on uniform-sized paper that is prepunched for two- or three-hole notebooks.

16. Record of Pastoral Calls and/or Counseling

The Pastoral Calls and/or Counseling form makes possible a record of the pastor's contacts with parish families and individuals. Little details, which mean so much in personal and purposeful ministry, are not forgotten if they are recorded.

The letter-sized forms can be kept in a two- or three-hole notebook or in the Family File folder. The pastor can write comments concerning each contact or put his comments on a dictating machine to be recorded by the secretary.

Each form provides space for name, address, phone,

date from first contact to last contact recorded on each sheet, page number, date of call, and individual contacted. There is plenty of room for recording comments about each contact.

17. Family Code Sheet

Person-to-person relationships are enhanced with emphasis upon efficiency in ministering to families. More time is available in personal ministry when time is saved in the area of administration. A code number for each family of the parish is extremely helpful, and the Family Code Sheet makes this possible.

A separate sheet is used for each letter of the alphabet. Thus, under A, the first family in alphabetic order would be A–1; the second, A–3, and so on. (Using every other number leaves space for the addition of new names.) In like manner, all families would be alphabetized and coded. For instance, W–12 might be a family that joined the congregation six months after the master code was developed, a family whose last name begins with a W and alphabetically was the seventh W family in the parish.

An example of the use of the code can be found in the pastor's suggestions for personal contact. He may refer to D–17 and make the following comment: "They have not been in worship for about six weeks and the father has been ill." The secretary or another responsible person checks the identity of D–17 and then uses the Personal Concern form to list name, address, and the other essential information and comments.

Another example of the advantages of family coding can be seen in making contacts for a banquet for those 65 and over. The pastor or someone who would know who

FAMILY CODE SHEET

First Letter of Family Name _____

Date this list prepared _____ _____ _____
                                                         mo.   day   yr.

Code	Family	Code	Family
1.		41.	
2.		42.	
3.		43.	
4.		44.	
5.		45.	
6.		46.	
7.		47.	
8.		48.	
9.		49.	
10.		50.	
11.		51.	
12.		52.	
13.		53.	
14.		54.	
15.		55.	
16.		56.	
17.		57.	
18.		58.	
19.		59.	
20.		60.	
21.		61.	
22.		62.	
23.		63.	
24.		64.	
25.		65.	
26.		66.	
27.		67.	
28.		68.	
29.		69.	
30.		70.	
31.		71.	
32.		72.	
33.		73.	
34.		74.	
35.		75.	
36.		76.	
37.		77.	
38.		78.	
39.		79.	
40.		80.	

Family Code Sheet

these individuals would be would go through the Family Record forms and give the code numbers of all those to be contacted. Then the name, address, and phone of the concerned parishioners would be typed or written on the Responsibility form. One copy of this list would be given to the person responsible for the phoning and a carbon copy provided for the general chairman of the event.

Family Code sheets are much faster and easier than saying or writing names. Also, in instances where names are similar, the code always designates the right family. The general chairman of the Annual Every Member Canvass will find the coding of families of great help.

Family coding should be updated as often as necessary. A large, growing, changing church may want to do this annually. A smaller, more stable congregation may find every three or four years to be sufficient. At least two copies of the coding sheets should be made in order to provide a master file and a carbon as a working copy. In some churches, several copies are desirable.

18. The Pastor's Personal Programing

The Pastor's Personal Programing material enables him to see each day at a glance. The working day is divided into half-hour periods. There are sections on the page where he can indicate the time for devotions, reading and study, visiting in the hospital or homes of the parishioners, counseling, attending meetings, making phone calls, writing letters, and so on. There is space for listing miscellaneous tasks to be done and for general notes and thoughts.

Time becomes much more productive when used wisely and to best advantage. This can only be done through planning. Every pastor should plan his work and should work from his plan. Every congregation should want to help their pastor in this area. There is nothing more expensive than wasted time, and wise indeed are the pastor and congregation when they seek always to "redeem the time."

19. Church Record Book

A forty-year summary of the vital statistics of a congregation can be entered in the Church Record Book. This is not a book where the names of those baptized, married, and the like are entered. It is but a summary of these activities. For instance, one enters the number of baptisms for 1968, marking how many were adult baptisms and how many were children. Many churches want to record this information so they can compare one year with another.

There is a place for recording attendance totals, finances, weddings, funerals, membership, and baptisms. A year's contributions or a year's attendance can be seen at a glance; there is room on a single page to record this information. There is a separate line for each of the fifty-two weeks. Thus, it is easy to check the contributions or attendance for the thirty-second Sunday of the current year with the corresponding Sunday of past years. There is also a running total column for such data. The Church Record Book gives an overview of congregational activity and growth.

20. Christian Budget Book

Millions of budget books are purchased each year, but none are specifically designed for guidance in Christian stewardship. The Church constantly teaches stewardship of time, talent, and treasure. The Christian Budget Book gives tangible evidence of Christian guidance in the wise use of these three sacred commodities.

The Christian Budget Book provides space for recording the expenditures of the year, income, monthly and annual totals, major tax deductions, suggestions for planning to participate in church activities, vacation and camp dates, and other suggestions for spiritual growth.

The Christian Budget Book is an excellent tool for teaching the proper concepts of Christian stewardship. It should be made available for newlyweds, new church members, and all other families of the parish. It is an excellent tool for every family receiving offering envelopes.

Conclusion

The world will not be won for Christ by those who are unwilling or unable to spend time with individuals. The Church will never become what it should be unless there are those willing to do the routine jobs as well as the glamorous ones.

Much of what can be done through the use of the tools described in this chapter will not be seen by most of the congregation, and those who assume these responsibilities will not be in the limelight.

The small investment necessary to secure and use these adequate and needed tools is meager compared to what is accomplished for the Kingdom. Any congregation that has invested in the leadership of pastors, secretaries, and other staff members should realize the necessity of making a small investment in those things that make church administration more efficient, economical, and effective. These tools put hands and feet to the prayers of thousands who desire and need the person-to-person relationship which only the Church can give.

Five

Personnel for
Personal Concern

This chapter is devoted to ways to secure, enthuse, and retain personnel to help bring "new life" and personal concern to a congregation. Creative churchmanship can best be practiced or promoted by those who are devoted to this end. Every congregation must constantly be enlisting, training, and inspiring leadership. This demands more than a temporary spirit of enthusiasm; it must be a concerted and constant effort toward devotion and faithfulness.

The Sacredness of All Life

Believers need a sharpened insight concerning the inspiration derived from participating in the details of congregational life. They must be taught that it is as sacred to work and help in the office as it is to teach a church school class. Also, all should realize that Christian service is not merely participating in the life of the church directly, but that it is anything done for the good of man and to the glory of God. It is not a sin to serve in a community drive, with the Girl Scout movement, in a fund-raising for medical research, on a social service board, or in any of the many similar endeavors. Doctrinal and theological bases should be given more pointedly to individuals so that they do not feel guilty about taking time from their own local church efforts to serve other worthy causes. If all of life is sacred, the Lord wants us to participate in every way possible in that which is meaningful. This does not mean that we can do everything at the same time, but throughout life variety should be part of our effort to help mankind.

In the life of the Church there are those who would place being a missionary, a pastor, a capable teacher, or the leader of a prayer meeting above other talents necessary for the local congregation to have a strong program. Yet, it is no more sacred to be able to do these things than it is to chair a committee, help in the kitchen, or work in the office. The opportunity to stress this is present every time a person is asked to help in his church. A meeting held to inform him of what is expected of him in his position should devote some time in presenting theological soundness to his service. Volunteers for creative churchmanship and emphasis upon personal concern for all members will be strengthened and encouraged if the calling to this is seen to be as important as any other area of church activity. All of life should be lived to the glory of God. The chapel, sanctuary, prayer room, or roller skating rink are all places where God is present and life should be lived acknowledging that He is Lord at all times.

Every One a Minister

All of life is sacred and every believer is a minister. Some churches stress this. They show on their bulletin each week the name of their pastor or pastors; they also list *"Ministers—the Entire Membership."* This graphically illustrates a proper perspective of pastor and people. Every believer should realize to the fullest his privileges in Christ. He constantly exerts influence, not only when he is in the church building, but wherever he may be. Christianity is not a band of professionals, but believers bound together through the love of Christ.

There are leaders and followers. Some men are good at one thing, some at another, and each has a gift differing from the other. But the call to commitment is extended to all. It is one of the tasks of the Church to make certain that this call is realized to its fullest.

The Involvement of All Age Groups

The total creative church program must involve the united efforts of all members of a congregation; the program is not complete and cannot be fulfilled if all ages are not kept in mind.

The last generation put emphasis on youth work. This is fine and should not be neglected. Nevertheless, recent years have shown beyond a doubt that youth work suffers unless adults are intimately involved in it. There can be no strong church without strong adult leadership. Many people are more than willing that the next generation be converted, but it is the present generation of adults which must be reached with the Christian message. If this is done, the chances of the next generation's living devotedly for Christ are greatly increased.

The Church is not a club one joins. The Church is wherever believers are, any moment of any day. The specific activities of any church program should be aimed to help individuals to live to the glory of Christ wherever they find themselves.

An illustration of the interaction of adults, youth, and

children can be seen in mission emphasis. The Church is mission. Specific activities should emphasize this. Perhaps a mission festival is to be observed. This should not be the responsibility of a few women in the church, but should be a part of a total church program. Adults should be involved in planning meetings along with youth and children. Promotion for the event might include whatever ordinary means of publicity a church uses as well as posters that the children could make. If the mission theme was India, children and youth alike could be involved in recreation, study, and worship around this theme. Guest speakers could be scheduled to appear before meetings where the entire family would be present. The use of money given to support these efforts could be explained to all ages of the congregation. In this way, many more people would be exposed to the Church in mission than if only a few did all the work.

The same things can be said about office work. Many people should know what needs doing in the office and how their talents could be used. There is no reason why children, youth, and adults could not help with the details of church administration. More about this will be stated later.

The Treasure Chest of Talent

Every church has individuals who can capably serve in some capacity. Individuals are needed as teachers, officers, to make personal calls, to serve on committees, to help in the office, to help with Vacation Church School, and in many other activities. Even while we emphasize the needs of the local congregation, appreciation should be extended to those who serve in worthy causes outside the local program.

There have been many books written about training teachers and other officers. The remainder of this chapter will emphasize the securing of office help for creative church-manship. There is much to be done here and most churches could accomplish much if they tried. Every church has available those who can type, file, answer phones, record financial giving, look after the details of the library, and so on. The problem lies in securing these people, a problem which takes consistent promotion and constant training.

Securing and Training Office Help

One of the most important points in securing office help is letting the need be known. A general statement that help is needed in the office is usually of little avail; needs must be stated specifically to the entire congregation through every publicity medium possible.

The training of volunteers must be specific and complete. The pastor, other staff members, or a responsible committee must make certain that volunteer help has received sufficient guidance to do a job well and to feel at ease with it. All materials to do the job efficiently should be available when help arrives. Far too often, churches put thousands of dollars into building a plant and then neglect the instruments for efficient work in the office. Individuals who have modern conveniences at home are discouraged if they must work with inadequate equipment at their church.

It must be realized there will be a large turnover of volunteer office personnel. This is true in any area of church life. Check the list of committee members of your church three years ago and you will be amazed at how many different ones are on the same committees today. Church school teachers are constantly changing. This is due not only to the mobile population of our nation, but also to disinterest, to a lack of training or dedication, and to a host of other reasons. Constantly and consistently, office help must be enlisted and trained. Remember, if congregations put forth half the time and effort securing volunteer office workers that they do securing volunteer teachers, committee members and chairmen, choir members, and so forth, they would have an abundance of office help. The importance of office workers must be stressed time and again. The parish letter, the pulpit, individual comments should all be used to full advantage in letting the congregation know the value of these services. All other aspects of a congregational program are strengthened by better office administration, thus enhancing the value of office volunteers.

Appreciation to the volunteers in the office can include letters from the pastor or other staff members, an appreciation dinner annually, a listing of their names along with teachers and other workers in the annual program or other promotional material.

The relationship between the volunteer worker and the staff is very important. The staff must realize that volunteers will never replace any of them. If the church program were not full, it would have no need of staff at all. The greater and more complex a program becomes, the more staff is required. The more volunteers who are willing to help, the greater need there will be of staff. Program participation and financial backing are greater when people have a tangible part in it and it meets a need in their lives and the lives of others.

Good equipment must be provided for staff as well as volunteer help. A modern church certainly should have good office equipment. An efficient mimeograph machine is a necessity; churches that can afford to do so would profit from the purchase of an offset printing machine. The initial expense is more than that of a mimeograph, but the results are better. A folding machine, an electric stapler, an addressograph machine, and adequate dictating equipment are also essential. Sufficient filing cabinets and storage space add to the pleasure of office work. The materials used for recording finances and other information concerning families of the congregation, correspondence, and every other aspect of promotional life should be the best available. The goal is to run a church office that is as efficient and economical as possible. Every minute saved is a minute that can be devoted to other worthwhile duties. Every penny saved is money that can be devoted to other work in the Kingdom of God.

There should be a schedule of the office activities and of those who will be helping with them. This should be planned as far in advance as possible. Some individuals will want to designate a specific day or half a day of the week on which they can regularly come to the office, while others will be on call when needed. Office routine should be put down on paper as a guide to securing the necessary volunteers. The time for recording financial giving, publishing the parish letter, marking attendance, typing letters, and so on can be ascertained well ahead of time.

It is amazing how much is done willingly when members are encouraged to help. Volunteers of one local congregation have for years sent a weekly parish letter to about five hundred families, with paid staff spending less than three hours a week on it. Volunteers mimeograph, fold, insert enclosures, address, staple, tie in bundles, and do all other things necessary for the mailing. Another weekly church mailing to approximately four hundred families is done entirely by volunteers, including the gathering of the news and typing of the stencils.

There is no church that is not helped when volunteer office workers are used effectively and efficiently. Several volunteers make light and quick work of a tremendous task.

Some Specific Suggestions for Volunteer Office Help

There are several specific ways in which volunteer office help can be an asset to a local congregation. Several of these relate to the pastor and his workload. Most pastors are burdened with administrative details; they have little time for the personal ministry that is so needed today. Therefore, some suggestions to help the pastor:

First, it might be said that volunteers can do much in the pastor's study. Volunteers can keep magazines and other materials in an orderly fashion. The pastor's office *can* be kept neat if there is someone in the parish willing to apply himself in this area. Once he is told where things go, he can tidy up and save precious minutes for the pastor.

Second, wise is the pastor who preserves the fruit of his wide reading. Often there are articles and comments that he desires to keep. Yet, it is time-consuming to develop and maintain a filing system. This is something willing volunteers can do. The pastor can designate where items are to be filed and volunteers can cut them out and place them in their proper category. Only a few seconds are required to mark items for filing, but much time is needed to cut them out and paste them into the file. There are several good filing systems available and the purchase of one for the pastor is a good investment by a congregation.

The filing system is further enhanced when sermon books are indexed. A separate sheet is maintained for every chapter of the Bible; materials pertaining to this chapter are pasted or written on these pages, and all sermons by the many different authors can be filed by chapter and verse, code number of the book, and page number of the sermon. Thus, in thirty seconds, a pastor can determine whether or not a sermon on any particular chapter or verse of the Bible is among his books. Volunteers are more than willing to do this original research and filing. It saves time and enriches a pastor's study efforts.

Every book in the pastor's library should be coded for quick and easy reference. The pastor's reading can be preserved by volunteers who will type the code number of the book, page number, and designated material to be filed. Volunteers willing to type the material and file it save the time of getting the book from the library shelf to seek out the needed reference. If a book is from the public library, mark lightly with a pencil the portions to be typed and erase the pencil marks after typing is done.

A retired couple of one church does this work at home for their pastor. They appreciate doing it and it is a tremendous help to him. The pastor's reading is preserved for future reference with very little effort on his part.

A pastor should properly file not only his reading material but also his original thoughts. These thoughts can be put on a dictating machine and typed off by volunteers and filed. It is amazing how many good sermon starters and illustrative thoughts come; if they are recorded at the moment, they prove very helpful. This enlarges one's ministry and enriches one's messages.

The typing from books or of original thoughts can be done on good-quality sheets of letter-sized paper. Between quotations leave three spaces, so that each item can be cut and pasted in the proper place in the files.

The Dictating Machine

The modern pastor should take advantage of the convenience of a dictating machine. It can be used for letters, recording original thoughts, referring a secretary to material to be typed from a particular book, recording comments of calls on parishioners, giving direction to individuals, making comments to be typed on the quarterly reports of families of the church, giving assignments of personal contacts in the homes, dictating sermons to be typed before being preached, recording important meetings, recording sermons at time of delivery, and a host of other possibilities.

The initial cost of a dictating machine is small compared to its benefits. Even greater efficiency is possible if a portable machine is available for the pastor. Some portables can be carried in one's pocket. They produce tone of fine fidelity and can be used in conjunction with the office dictating machine. There are many times in every day in which a portable dictating machine could be used to increase a pastor's efficiency in personal concern for families of the congregation.

Volunteer workers can type what has been recorded on the dictating machine. On occasion, there may be letters or other materials that the pastor would not want anyone else to see or hear and this he can type himself; if it is a staff situation, the secretary can do it. The pastor must use discretion on what the volunteers may type from his dictating machine, but the chances of getting into problems here are slim and what is to be gained far outweighs the disadvantages of using volunteers.

The Program Coordinator

Churches with large membership and staff may desire to secure a paid coordinator for their program. His responsibility would be to integrate the complex church program and skillfully and efficiently use volunteer help. He should not be expected to be an expert in every area, but an individual who gets along well with others and who has a total grasp of what the congregation is endeavoring to do. Frequently, the coordinator's working day covers the afternoon through the evening. This enables him to attend committee meetings and other evening activities. A coordinator strives to arrive at efficiency in church administration. Getting all the details together is of utmost importance and most congregations would profit by having this done. If no paid help is available in this area, volunteer help should be considered to assume the responsibility of coordination in order to relieve the pastor of many time-consuming details. The pastor is trained for teaching, preaching, and pastoral ministry, and should not be sentenced to mimeographing and routine office work. His investment in training, and the financial investment of the congregation supporting him, is wasted to a large extent if administrative details constitute the bulk of his activities. Creative churchmanship is best achieved when the pastor is free to be a pastor and the laity are willing to assume responsibilities to the best of their abilities.

The personnel for personal concern can be procured if a congregation plans its work and works its plan. The goal is ". . . for the perfecting of the saints, for the work of the ministry, for the edifying of the body of Christ: till we all come in the unity of the faith, and of the knowledge of the Son of God, unto a perfect man, unto the measure of the stature of the fulness of Christ . . ." (Eph. 4: 12, 13).

Six

Propelled by
the Positive

Once we have interested people in personal concern for others, we must provide them with a purposeful and tangible program through which their concern can be expressed. We who believe Christ died for the world must use every creative means possible to manifest this message to mankind.

Every effort of the Church, be it corporate worship, social activity, prayer service, or committee meeting, should be Christ-oriented. We must do more than *say* we are lifting up Christ; we must *do* it. Many congregations are caught in stultifying church routine, and they both need and desire guidance to vitality. They want their church to be a station where the struggling soul can be filled with solace and strength. Spectacular victories are won on battlefields, but there must be a West Point to train leaders of the men in the field. The local congregation must be this West Point, a place to train, to encourage, and to help. New life must profit from the past and be challenged by the present and the future. It will not be ushered in through the burning down of all church edifices and abolishing all organizational patterns.

It is impossible for any one person or program to solve

all the Church's problems. Materials and programs are guidelines to be adapted and molded to the needs of a local church and community. The suggestions in this section are made in the hope that, used with discretion and diligence, they too may help bring new life to congregations. These suggestions are not daydreams; they have been tried and tested with enthusiastic response and have not outlived their usefulness.

CORPORATE WORSHIP

A few years ago during vacation we worshiped in different congregations of different denominations for three consecutive Sundays. One more Sunday in the pew and I would have been a backslider. The services were cold, indifferent, and irrelevant.

Sunday morning corporate worship can be an invigorating experience. The congregation can sing with sincerity, appreciate Scripture intelligently interpreted, and respond to a sermon speaking to our day. These things alone will help start new life in a congregation.

Pure worship is not attained through the removal of everything from the worship service that speaks to human need. It is no less sacred to present a message that speaks to the needs of people than one that deals with theological jargon. God has no objection if people enjoy the service and participate with enthusiasm. The pastor is such an important factor in the worship service; from him must flow warmth, dedication, and enthusiasm. His words should seek to educate and enlighten those present. He is not called to lambast, but to lead others to full commitment to Christ. His task is not always to tell what is wrong with the Church, but to give positive guidance for its betterment and for individual Christian growth. Of what help is the pastor who berates his congregation because of their indifference and then rushes home, himself, to watch the Sunday football game on TV? It is easy to single out and singe the sinners, but difficult to stir individuals to seek and see the Saviour. The worship service is a time of stimulating instruction and should be free of superfluous distractions. The amount of time invested in such a service is fantastic. If there are three hundred people present, this is equivalent to the pastor's spending thirty ten-hour days with each person individually. Every second of corporate worship should be used judiciously. The congregation should be educated to its content and purpose. They need instruction in doctrine and Scripture, and in the application of these to their daily living. Thus, observances of special days and emphasis in worship must be well planned and personalized. This is true whether it be for Girl Scout Sunday, to honor the high school and college graduates, or to welcome visitors to the service.

Sermon Outline Made Available to Families of the Parish

If families of the parish receive the sermon outline by mail each week, they have time to meditate upon it and the suggested Scripture. It is amazing how much more enriching the experience of worship is when the parish is acquainted with the pastor's subject matter in advance.

There is no merit in the pastor's presenting a "surprise" package each Sunday. He may have prepared his sermon for hours, but it is too much to expect the congregation to absorb the fruits of his labors in twenty minutes. He may glory in his oratorical skill, but he will soon discover that the congregation is learning pitifully little.

Let me speak from experience. I was inspired by one

professor of college days who always lectured without notes. He presented his materials to the class meaningfully and apparently "off the cuff." We became close friends, and one day he revealed to me that his entire lecture was in his inside coat pocket. He was well prepared, but he had put the content in his cranium for off-the-cuff presentation to the class. This so intrigued me that I put forth effort to present my sermons in this fashion. I took pride in developing my message and then speaking without notes. The eye contact was constant and the impression on individuals initially rewarding. Nonetheless, it finally dawned upon me that, although I had the outline memorized, the congregation did not. The ratio of congregational knowledge to my hours of preparation was very poor. It was in this period that I began the "mailed outline" method.

An outline cannot impart all of a message, but it is helpful, especially so when pertinent Scriptures are listed. Some of my congregation kept every outline for future reference and study. Thus, information gleaned from a series of messages on a particular book of the Bible, problems of the day, or general biblical theme could be studied in greater depth. It was a profitable venture both for me and for the congregation. One positive by-product for me was the discipline of a Wednesday-morning deadline for my sermon outline. It certainly took the pressure off last-minute-Saturday sermon preparation. This in itself proved to me the merit of the mailed outline.

Sermon Stimulants

There are other steps that make a message more pertinent and practical to the congregation. The suggestion was made to me, "Let us discuss the message before it is preached." It was a dare, but it ended up as a dynamic catalyst destined to develop my relationship to the congregation more than I had ever dreamed possible.

For several years before this suggestion we had frequently spent time at the midweek service endeavoring to discuss the message of the previous Sunday. Those present were given opportunity to ask questions, make comments, and appraise the previous Sunday's message. This was helpful, but I must admit it was almost impossible to elicit much response. The message had been preached. The "Lord" had spoken. There was little more to be said about it; it was difficult to develop any meaningful discussion. There was no strong reaction one way or the other.

However, when I began presenting each Wednesday night my tentative outline for the message to be delivered a week and a half later, an entirely different reaction resulted. Usually I would begin by saying, "If you had twenty minutes to talk about this portion of Scripture, what would you say? What about this subject do you feel would be most helpful to those present?" The midweek crowd came alive; beautiful insights and illustrations were often forthcoming. They responded to what I was planning to do with greater freedom and enthusiasm than they ever did with what I had already preached. The discussion also revealed to me where knowledge was lacking, practical application needed strengthening, and interest was present. And the weaknesses of my sermon outline became evident. I do not recall one sermon outline presented to the people ten days before delivery that I did not change in some way. Some outlines I completely discarded and started over.

Those who participated in preparing the sermon listened to its presentation more attentively. They were thrilled when some point they had suggested was emphasized. They listened for discussed illustrations, ideas, and suggestions. My fear of lost interest if individuals knew what was to be preached was ill-founded.

It was most helpful to have considered controversial social issues with thirty to fifty members of the congregation before preaching the message concerning them. The sympathetic and prayerful group made the impact of such messages greater and at the same time less divisive. In a sense, it was the people's message that was proclaimed and not just the pastor's.

Personalized Worship Folders

It was interesting to hear one reaction to the question "Have you ever been told that you remind soneone of a famous person?" One individual replied, "I am a famous person. I am myself. I am the only me in the whole world."

This is terrific theology. We, too often, piously play down our own importance. Jesus never did. He said each person was worth more than the entire world. It is no tribute to one's humility to say, "I am nothing, and worse than a worm." Each person is important in the sight of God and to himself. How can one love his neighbor if he does not love himself? How can one really appreciate God if he does not accept the truth that God thinks he is important? This emphasis is not playing upon sympathy or catering to the whims of individuals. It is a fact of life; it fosters spiritual growth.

The weekly worship folder should convey this concept of the individual's worth. Most churches have accepted the use of the worship folder, but to this day most confine it to those who are present for the corporate worship experience.

Every family in the parish should have opportunity to know the order of service before arriving for corporate worship. There is really no need of a parish letter and also a Sunday morning worship folder. The weekly mailing should include the order of service for Sunday morning, sermon outline, announcements, and pertinent congregational information. The ill, shut-ins, families on vacation, those whose employment involves Sunday work, etc., should all be kept current of church news. Many people appreciate studying the sermon outline, offering the prayers, even singing the hymns at home.

The sermon outline and order of worship should appear on the same page of the weekly parish letter. Extra copies of this page should be printed for Sunday morning distribution to visitors and to families of the parish who have forgotten to bring their mailed copy.

There is no reason why the mailed bulletin cannot be as beautiful as the worship folders. Many churches have an artist's sketch of their church or a beautiful full-color picture of the church building or nave on the front.

The more personal in information and appearance the weekly parish letter is, the more meaningful it becomes to the congregation. The Kingdom of God is much advanced through personal concern. The well-prepared weekly mailed church letter is one channel through which to do this.

Remember that the weekly mailing can be a medium for education. Tracts, pamphlets, mimeographed material can be enclosed each week. The material available today for Christian training is fantastic. The misuse and failure to use this material is appalling. Variety should be sought in choosing enclosures. Don't load every issue with prods for giving and tracts on tithing. Inform, inspire, and ignite the soul, and finances will be forthcoming.

MULTIPLE SERVICES

Modern living makes it necessary for members of the congregation to be given several opportunities for corporate worship each week. America is no longer a nation of farmers who work six days and reserve the seventh for necessary chores and worship. It is a complex society and becoming more so daily. No longer do high school graduates choose from a few vocations; they must face the frustrations of one decision among thousands. Factories work three shifts, seven days each week. Individuals work all hours of the day and night; some have different days off each week, and a constant changing of working hours.

It is ridiculous to expect all church members to be able to attend corporate worship service at any one particular hour. Even if all wanted to attend, it would be impossible for some to do so. Our spiritual ego may be fed when many are together at one time and we need not submit to the embarrassment of a service with few in attendance, but the needs of the congregation must be met. A congregation has its head in the sand if it believes that all members could come to Sunday morning worship service if they really wanted. What does this say to the Sunday worker—to the electrician, the phone company installer, the radio announcer? How does this meet the needs of the workers in restaurants, where thousands of churchgoers regularly eat after services? It speaks of a wrong interpretation of New Testament teaching. It speaks of a deadness in the congregation unwilling to put forth initiative and creativity to provide varied times and types of worship services.

Churches of several hundred members should have at least two services every Sunday morning. The attendance at each will be less than when only one service is held, but the grand total will always be more. Negligence may be a reason for nonattendance at Sunday corporate worship for many, but absolute impossibility is the reason for some. These people should not be forgotten. A Sunday evening service would be of value in some congregations.

Midweek Service

Services should be provided throughout the week for those not able to attend on Sunday. The now practically extinct midweek prayer service did serve a purpose. Revival of it is not requested, but some type of meaningful midweek service should be offered. For those who cannot attend worship on Sunday, this is an opportunity to meet with believers; for those who do come on Sunday, it is a strength and help. The format of the midweek service will vary from congregation to congregation; it may be a prayer service, healing service, study group, discussion group, or the like.

Holy Communion

The Sacrament of Holy Communion has rightfully been receiving more emphasis in recent years. It is a reflection upon congregational leadership that many members go months without an opportunity to receive the sacraments. Their work or another legitimate reason may prevent attendance at the stated Communion service. Frequently no other opportunity is offered to them, and they are reluctant to ask the pastor to bring Communion to their home.

Holy Communion can be served on Sunday night, at a healing service, midweek service, in the home, on retreat, and elsewhere. The worship associated with the reception of the Sacrament, wherever and whenever it may be held, can be very meaningful. Even following a social gathering and while still sitting at the table, the Holy Communion service can be meaningful and most helpful.

Small Groups

Groups can be effective at any hour of the week that is convenient for a few or many to assemble. The time and place are not of particular importance, but believers should be challenged to meet, to study, to pray, and to share together. Even the elderly and shut-ins can have believers come to their home once a week. The infirm have a responsibility to invite believers, just as much as believers have a responsibility to call upon such members of the congregation. Shut-ins should not simply rejoice that different individuals come to visit, or, as is more often the case, lament that no one ever comes; they must face the responsibility they have to open their home to believers. This helps them feel very much a part of the congregation even though they are unable to come to the building erected for congregational use. They are still very much a part of the Church. A Holy Communion service with a shut-in and several other believers present is a blessing to all participating.

RETREATS

Personal concern for individuals must include opportunities for them to get really acquainted with others. Loneliness is prevalent in our society, and many people have no purposeful relationships either with God or with man. They are alone in a world of activity and population boom. The widespread retreat movement of our day is a phenomenon designed to help combat this purposelessness.

A retreat is not necessarily a move away from the world, but simply the temporary removal of oneself from the hustle and bustle of everyday modern living. *Retreat* is not even the best word to describe this experience, for it results in an advance for Christ and for one's ability to face and solve one's problems. It is not a retreat from life, but a momentary shifting of emphasis that can make all of life more meaningful. There are several directions that a daring congregation can take regarding retreats.

The Family Retreat

An entire family can be drawn closer together when all members participate in a retreat. They are able to experience jointly the atmosphere of the retreat; when they return home, the spirit caught there will continue as they share with one another. This combats the problem that can arise when an individual returns home from a retreat enthused at what he has discovered, only to find that other members of the family could not care less. He may be walking on cloud nine, but they are still in the valley of decision with their own problems. He may have had a heavenly vision, but other members of his family or those with whom he works cannot appreciate the dynamics of his spiritual victories. It is impossible to carry back the experiences of a retreat to others, as impossible as it would be to carry back the concept that sweeps over an individual as he views the Grand Canyon. You have to experience it yourself in order to get the impact. There is no substitute for common experiences in the developing of family harmony.

Couples' Retreat

There are occasions when it is good for husband and wife to attend a retreat. The problems common to married life and rearing a family usually constitute the bulk of discussion and consideration on such occasions. It provides a time for couples to pause and refresh their relationships to God and to one another. The responsibilities of work and family are removed for a day or two and new perspective can be gained by both.

The director of a couples' retreat should be able to speak to the needs of husbands and wives. It is well if he is adept at marriage counseling as well as mature and wise in the Christian faith.

Men's or Women's Retreats

There are times when it is good for men and women to be alone. Such occasions should not be held to the neglect of couples' and family retreats, but should supplement them.

Senior-High and Junior-High Retreats

Youth especially appreciate retreats and respond favorably to them. A good retreat is worth a year of the average church school class to most youth. Youth retreats should be often, varied, and challenging.

Where to Hold Retreats?

There are many retreat centers available. Included among them would be local church camps, conference and synod sites, interdenominational campgrounds, state and national parks, trailer camps, private campsites, farms, and spacious private homes. Every church could have access to at least one of these places. Search your area and you will discover several places available for your retreats.

Give consideration to your own church facilities for retreats. They may not be ideal, but many church areas can be adapted for rewarding retreat experiences. Those attending can come to the church for lectures and discussion and return home for the night. However, they may even choose to sleep in the church all night. This is especially true if it is a young people's retreat.

If the congregation's buildings are totally inadequate, there may be a neighborhood church willing to share its facilities with another church.

Suggested Schedule for a Weekend Retreat

FRIDAY:

3:00 P.M.	Arrival of leader and those in charge of arrangements
5:30 P.M.	Evening meal for all able to be present
8:00 P.M.	Orientation, group singing, presentation of purpose of the retreat
8:30 P.M.	Lecture by the retreat director
9:00 P.M.	Small-group discussion (no more than eight per group)
10:30 P.M.	Free time
11:00 P.M.	Devotional period

SATURDAY:

7:15 A.M.	Private devotional time
8:00 A.M.	Breakfast
9:30 A.M.	Lecture by the retreat director
10:00 A.M.	Small-group discussion
11:30 A.M.	Free time
NOON.	*Lunch*
1:30 P.M.	Corporate prayer led by the retreat director
2:00 P.M.	Group discussion
3:00 P.M.	Free time for reading, hiking, rest, etc.
5:00 P.M.	Dinner
6:45 P.M.	Song time
7:15 P.M.	Lecture by retreat director
8:00 P.M.	Group discussion

| 9:30 P.M. | Free time and snacks |
| 10:30 P.M. | Devotional period |

SUNDAY:

7:00 A.M.	Holy Communion
8:00 A.M.	Breakfast
9:45 A.M.	Worship
11:45 A.M.	Dinner
1:00 P.M.	Sharing time and evaluation period
2:15 P.M.	Homeward bound

A retreat does not answer all the problems of those attending, but it can benefit the majority if it is well planned. The first service should be at an hour when all have arrived. Those able to come early should care for as many details as possible. Don't strive for the "perfect" retreat. A well-thought-out schedule is helpful, but it should not be adhered to as the "law of the Medes and Persians." The director and participants should maintain a spirit of flexibility.

Retreat Orientation

State the purpose of the retreat at the beginning. Do this prayerfully and with specific guidance to help individuals grasp immediately why they are at the retreat and the goals hoped to be attained.

Devotional Spirit

The devotional spirit is necessary for a successful spiritual retreat. Don't waste so much time with the mechanics of meeting the needs of food and lodging that the devotional atmosphere is neglected. The director's first lecture should be a challenge; it need not be a sermon.

If you are fortunate to be at a retreat center where employees care for meals and dishes, more time will be available for discussion and retreat activities. Nevertheless, retreat participants having to do the cooking and washing up does not detract from the retreat if work is done in the proper spirit and done efficiently. A committee should be given the responsibility for scheduling cooking, dishwashing, cleaning tables, and so forth. Don't waste retreat time deciding who is going to do what and when. Ask everyone to cooperate with the suggestions of the kitchen committee.

Getting Started

The first group discussion should be stimulated by the director's remarks and should be a time for getting acquainted and considering the reasons for attending a retreat. Each individual should consider such questions as: Why did he come to the retreat? What does he hope to gain from participating? What does he hope to contribute to the retreat? How does he feel he can most gain from this experience? Where is he now in his religious pilgrimage?

Each discussion group should number not less than four nor more than eight. A convener should be designated for each group. He is not expected to be an expert in small-group dynamics, but serves simply as the catalyst for group discussion. Lectures and resource materials enrich these discussion periods. Resource materials are especially helpful if they are sent to the participants prior to the retreat for their perusal and study.

Rest

The retreat should be designed to refresh the body as well as the soul. It is best to endeavor not to return from a retreat so exhausted you are of no value to your family or employer. The exciting things you have experienced mean little to them. They only see your outward countenance and behavior. Exhaustion brings out the worst in anyone, and this condition rarely makes others enthusiastic to attend retreats. Those who need little sleep or who cannot sleep when away from home should respect others who can and do need rest.

Redeeming the Time

The hours of a retreat pass so quickly. It is best to have an unhurried schedule, but all must be encouraged to face each minute at depth. A relaxed and joyous spirit should pervade the weekend, but constant, frivolous talk should not be the order of the day.

Individuals must be encouraged to talk with one another at depth. This helps create a climate of love and willingness to love and to be loved, to share and to permit others to share, to seek and to reveal. Too often a retreat is about to end before an individual realizes he has frittered away his time and been false to himself and to others.

Lectures

The messages by the director set the pace for the retreat. They should be concise and relevant to the theme of the retreat and to the lives of those attending it. No message should be over thirty minutes in length. A few minutes after each lecture can be devoted to question-and-answer time before dispersing to small-group discussion. Clarification of points beforehand helps in small-group discussion.

Free Time

Free time is as valuable on a retreat as lectures, Bible study, and prayer. It gives opportunity for individuals to get better acquainted, for personal meditation and reading, for quiet time, for rest and relaxation. These are all on the plus side of a good retreat program.

Variety—The Spice of Retreats

Fun songs, Gospel songs, the great hymns of the Church, recreation, prayer, study, silent times, group discussion—all have their place on a retreat and should be interwoven in a program free from monotony. Each retreat should vary in emphasis as well as being well balanced in activities. Available copies of a hymnbook or camp song booklet stimulate the song service.

The Director

The success of a retreat is dependent to a large extent upon the preparations of the director. He must to the best of his ability anticipate the retreatants' needs. His lectures should be provocative and helpful. His choice of subject matter should not simply evoke discussion, but should inform and inspire.

Effective consideration of his presentation is best achieved by keeping the discussion groups the same throughout the retreat. Effort should be made to know a few at depth and not simply to cover a lot of material. Retreat is a time to be stimulated in spirit and not necessarily to have all the questions of life answered. The rapport established among permanent groups is usually best for accomplishing this end. If several people come and go throughout the retreat, it may be better to form new groups after each lecture. Several newcomers arriving at the same time can constitute a group of their own.

Retreats and Corporate Worship

Of course there is guidance and emphasis upon private devotions at a retreat, but the director should lead corporate worship as well. Creativity can abound here. There can be a different worship center for each service—a campfire, picture, fireplace, old rugged cross, a floating cross with lighted candles on the lake, common chalice and loaf of bread, and so on. Whatever is done should have meaning for those present and be very much a part of their feelings.

The closing worship service at a retreat is a good time for what I call a New Testament service. It is based upon the suggestions of I Corinthians 14:26. All are asked to participate in the service through sharing a prayer, song, Scripture quotation, personal witness, interpretation of a doctrine or Scripture passage, practical insight, special blessing received during the retreat, problem faced, or special concern. Moments of silence intersperse periods of spontaneous verbal responses. The service should be permitted to move freely as the Spirit leads. Spontaneity springs from the fact that individuals have been together for a sustained period of time. The responsibility of the director is to coordinate the service and not to preach a sermon. The length of the service may be a half hour or an hour and a half, according to the desire of those present and the interest they show.

The secret of a successful New Testament service is a leader who allows no one to monopolize the time and at the same time does not coerce anyone to respond. He prepares for the service by announcing the day before what procedure is to be followed. He explains that each should give thought to the service and what he feels he can contribute to it. He stresses that pre-thought does not rule out spontaneous comments during the service itself.

Closing the Retreat

Sunday's noon meal is followed by informal visiting and putting the finishing touches on packing for the trip home. This should be done before the sharing and evaluation session. There should first be a sharing of blessing, insights, help, and spiritual advances experienced by those making the retreat, and opportunity to state future goals.

Second, the session should evaluate the retreat. Each participant should feel free to express himself honestly. The convenience of the date; the programs; the impact and effectiveness of the director; these and all other aspects of the retreat should be scrutinized. No one should take offense at what is said or become inflated with pride. It is understood that no retreat is perfect. The chief purpose of the evaluation is to improve future retreats. Perhaps evaluation is of greatest value because it so vividly says we are not perfect—that our efforts do fall short of the glory of God—but that He blesses in our midst in spite of us.

Retreat Expenses

Retreats cost money. Rental of facilities, publicity, resource leaders, insurance, mimeographing of materials, and many other items add to the expense. Retreats are not nearly so costly as indifferent or inactive members, however.

The expenses of the director should be carefully considered. A man capable of directing a retreat certainly should be reimbursed a minimum of $25 to $100 a day over and above his travel and meal expenses. There is much more time involved in directing a retreat than simply putting in the hours. Capable leadership and a strong program are most productive, and wise is the church willing to pay the price for them.

The local church can help defray expenses of those attending a retreat. The spiritual return per dollar in retreat investment is greater than in almost any other church activity. It is amazing how much is invested in plants and in materials for Christian education and how often meager are the returns in learning and loyalty.

The potential for spiritual growth from retreats remains virtually untapped by most congregations. It is well to encourage participation in retreats and camps with other churches, presbytery, conference, synod, district, interdenominational effort, and the like. These should be supplements to local church efforts and not substitutes for them. Regardless of membership size a local church can at least on occasion have a retreat of its own. It will be stronger by so doing.

Retreats in a Church Building

The following suggested schedule is for a retreat held at one's own church building or at a nearby facility.

FRIDAY:

6:00 P.M.	Dinner at the church
7:00 P.M.	Statement of purpose and goals of the retreat
7:15 P.M.	Lecture by the retreat director
7:45 P.M.	Group discussion
9:15 P.M.	Free time and snacks
10:00 P.M.	Group devotions

SATURDAY:

10:00 A.M.	Devotions
10:15 A.M.	Lecture by retreat director
10:45 A.M.	Group discussion
12:15 P.M.	Free time
12:30 P.M.	Lunch
1:15 P.M.	Period of silence for meditation, reading, private prayer

1:45 P.M.   Lecture by the retreat director
2:15 P.M.   Group discussion
3:45 P.M.   Free time
5:00 P.M.   Dinner
6:00 P.M.   Song time
6:30 P.M.   Lecture by the retreat director
7:00 P.M.   Group discussion
8:30 P.M.   Free time and snacks
9:30 P.M.   Devotions

SUNDAY:
7:00 A.M.   Holy Communion
8:00 A.M.   Breakfast at the church
            Church School and Worship. The retreat director speaks
            at the worship service

NOON.   *Lunch*
1:15 P.M.   Sharing time and evaluation
2:15 P.M.   Closing devotions
2:30 P.M.   Homeward bound

The use of one's own church building does not nullify the results of a retreat. Strength comes from individuals' being together for a sustained period of time. There are some general comments concerning such efforts, although the insights stated earlier about retreats are also applicable.

Meals can be provided by church members, catered, or secured at a local restaurant. Worship experiences can be in the nave, chapel, classroom, fellowship hall, parlor, or wherever it is convenient and appropriate.

The closing Sunday afternoon service may be patterned after the New Testament service described above. Another idea for this closing service uses a fireplace. Provide each person with a slip of paper. Ask him to write down some aspect of life that he would change or remove. It may be an indifferent spirit, resentments, a moral problem, a specific sin, or any one of a multitude of problems. There is no public sharing of what each one writes, but at an appropriate time during the service each one deposits his paper upon the fire. The flames consume the paper and symbolically speak of the removal through spiritual power of this particular problem in one's life. Holy Communion may be observed at this time, also.

Some groups desire an early Holy Communion service and breakfast together on Sunday. This is especially true if the retreat is for youth or single young adults. Sunday dinner should also be shared. This helps to prepare for the evaluation period to follow.

Retreats using local church facilities are especially helpful for families unable to be away from home even for one or two nights. They provide an opportunity for a larger number of individuals to participate in a retreat. Participants can sleep at the church. Sleeping bags or army cots serve well for youth and venturesome adults. It is surprising what can be done with a church's facilities if ingenuity is pursued. Most churches can be used far more often and with far greater creativity than is now the case. Use them for retreats. This will also keep retreat costs at a minimum.

Reading Material

Always have good reading material available, both to be used during the retreat and to be purchased and taken home. Devotional classics, modern translations of Scripture, magazines, and mimeographed materials should be among the selections. Provide quiet periods when such materials can be used advantageously. A bibliography of materials helpful to Christian growth should be provided for each participant. In the days after the retreat, individuals can secure those books and magazines that especially appeal to them.

Fresh Fish

Every human avenue should be explored to get individuals to attend a retreat. Elders, trustees, church school teachers, class officers, organizational officers, junior-aged children, high school students, couples, men, women, senior citizens, and vacation church school teachers are natural groupings and sources for retreatants. Strive to involve a large percentage of the membership of the congregation in retreat efforts over a period of a few years. Retreats are not for the spiritually "elite." They are for everyone.

The natural saturation point of retreat participants in any congregation is soon achieved. Prayerful and purposeful planning is necessary to go beyond the point where the same ones are "retreating" all the time. One suggestion is to conduct an occasional retreat that no one can attend unless he brings with him a retreat recruit; that is, a person who has never attended a retreat. In large congregations a further requirement should be that the recruit be a member of the local church.

Nothing stymies retreat influence and induces staleness as rapidly as having the same few people taking advantage of retreats. Vitality lies with the fresh fish caught up with the enthusiasm of their first retreat.

Retreats should not necessarily be scheduled or postponed on the basis of numbers. Four or five individuals can find such an experience very helpful; sometimes a small number is even more effective. Retreats provide a marvelous opportunity for pastor and people to draw closer to one another and to God.

Fruitful Seasons for Retreats

A logical time for a retreat is the early fall. This launches the year's new program for the leaders, officers, teachers, and so on. It gives them an opportunity to withdraw for a while and give depth consideration to the things of the Spirit.

Another opportune time is at the beginning of the calendar year. Congregational responsibilities are a drain upon spiritual vitality and retreats replenish this power.

Each congregation must realize that there is no "ideal" time for a retreat. Making a retreat is a demanding and disciplined experience, often neglected for matters of far less importance. Fall, winter, spring, or summer is a good time for a retreat if there is a willing soul to care for the details. Don't wait for a "convenient" season. Do it.

The Pastor and Retreats

The congregation should give the pastor an opportunity to attend a retreat each year as a participant. He should not always be involved as a director or coordinator of retreats. A pastor needs a retreat himself from time to time. Congregations should grant the time and assume the expenses for their pastor's retreat. He too has feet of clay, and blessed is the congregation that never forgets this. The flock cannot remain devoted unless their shepherd keeps close to the Good Shepherd.

The pastor can serve as the director for many of the local church retreats. This is especially true if he happens to be new in the parish. It provides him with an opportunity to become better acquainted with families of the church, and they with him. There will come a time when it is best to secure guest directors for most of the retreats with the pastor serving as coordinator.

The alert congregation strives for several retreats each year with different emphases, held at a variety of places and times, and appealing to different age levels and interests.

CHURCH PARTNERS

People should feel at home in the congregation before and after membership. This is sometimes difficult. Some congregations assign a sponsor to each new member. The sponsor helps the new member become better acquainted with others of the parish and come to a better understanding of church life.

A more effective plan is what can be termed "church partners." This concept places some responsibility on the new member as well as on present members. It is more than assigning someone to shepherd a new member. The new member is asked to choose someone of the congregation to serve as his church partner. This choice is usually one who has meant something to him in his spiritual pilgrimage. It is not a committee assignment, but an individual choice. It is not the concept of a father looking after a child, the old looking after the new, but rather the bringing together of individuals who have something in common.

Church partners encourage one another in doctrine, participation in activities, deepening of the devotional life, the area of spiritual reading, and the facing of personal problems. They become better acquainted and grow together in spiritual matters. The new member is made to realize he has something to contribute to the present member and vice versa. It is a mutual responsibility and privilege. New members must realize that they are not to be coddled into Christian conformity, but are called to Christian commitment. They are responsible to God and man and must live accordingly.

One of the greatest by-products of the church-partner concept is the deep satisfaction of the one asked that another appreciates his Christian witness. Each one asked is pleasantly surprised, but I have never known such a request to be refused. Sometimes, individuals never considered qualified by a committee to sponsor a new member are asked to be a church partner by a person joining the Church. They usually perform splendidly in this capacity; one reason may be that they are already an influence in the life of the one asking them to serve. It demonstrates that one need not be an important officer or leader in a church to be appreciated as a fellow Christian.

An appointed sponsor often misses the mark because he does not "click" with the new member to whom he is assigned. Church-partner emphasis directly and indirectly teaches that each Christian must strive to live above reproach and that he is an example for those who are watching.

New members are not nearly so concerned about some things that the pastor and the membership committee may feel are important. They yearn for Christian concern; the mechanics they can learn as they grow in grace. Church partners show us that Christianity is more than minute understanding of Church organization. "Professional" sponsors, even if they have all knowledge of the mechanics of making new members feel at home, still may lack the touch of common concern and mutual interest that exists between one who has been chosen by a new member and who has agreed to be a church partner with him. The circle of concerned members is automatically widened with the church-partner approach.

Summary of the Church-Partner Concept

The new member makes the choice of his church partner.

The present member requested to serve as a church partner has the opportunity to accept or refuse the invitation.

The church partners are not publicly announced.

As partners, both the new member and the present member assume responsibilities. It is a willingness on the part of the "old" and the "new" to be mutually helpful in spiritual growth.

The partnership is for a minimum of six months.

Sometime during the six-month period the church partners meet at one of their homes for a period of discussion concerning Christian commitment. This could very well be a dinner meeting.

An explanation of the church-partner concept and procedures should be kept before the congregation and presented in detail to each group of new members.

COUNSELING

How can the needs of individuals be met today? One way is through counseling. It is time consuming but very productive; it often constitutes the bulk of a pastor's ministry.

Use the Laity

The most practical suggestion I have to make concerning a creative counseling program is the use of the laity to help in this area. They can lighten the counseling load of the pastor and often their efforts are most fruitful.

The laity can best function through small groups. The pastor should take advantage of the therapeutic power of small-group involvement. Wherever groups meet for specific needs, individuals with similar needs can be channeled into them. Sometimes new groups can be formed from individuals who express need. Such groups may meet for only a few times or continue for weeks, months, or years. No group need be eternal to be effective. Some groups die a natural death of disinterest while others are dissolved when the need is met.

One group was formed in this way. A young unmarried girl came to my office and said she was pregnant. What do you do in such situations? The proper social agency had been contacted to give guidance, but life is more than having the answers to the details of birth.

One of the questions I asked was, "Why did you come to a pastor?" I will never forget the very plain but pungent reply, "Because I am a Christian." She was a Christian girl deeply involved and seeking a solution. We discussed her situation and various approaches to the multitude of problems it had triggered. I knew that, in spite of the hours I might devote to her, she would gain most from participation in a group that would serve to undergird and help her in the months ahead. I asked if she would be willing to meet with others and explained my reasons for suggesting this and what would be involved. I pointed to the support a group can offer and how it helps to get beyond one's own problem.

She agreed to participate in the venture. No such group existed in the parish. In her presence I phoned a young mother and explained the situation to her. She was not a professional counselor and I was not asking her to do a professional job. I simply wanted her to befriend a girl who had come from another state to live with relatives until her baby had been delivered. The mother was apprehensive, but willing. The following Tuesday night they got together for their first meeting.

A few days later, a disturbed career girl came to my study. I phoned the same mother and said, "I have another young lady for you," and explained the circumstances. A short time after this, a girl in her late teens stopped in to see me. She was a Roman Catholic. Things at home were so rough that she had left to live for a while in another section of town with relatives. As she walked by our church the thought came to her that the pastor must live nearby. She knocked at the door of a neighbor who directed her to my study. We talked and I suggested she meet with the others. I again phoned the young mother; now she had three.

Each girl had unique problems but a common need and concern. It was not long before other girls were invited to meet with them. Tuesday nights became a time of sharing, praying, and fellowship for them. This group participation was not a "cure all," but an undergirding strength.

I saw each girl several times privately. I could have counseled with each hours on end, but I would not have accomplished what a few times alone and many hours in the group did. They needed not only the listening ear of the pastor, but also a group that would accept them as persons. Apparent defeat turned into victory.

Sometimes an existing group can minister to a specific need, as I will illustrate. A mother phoned to inquire about our church; the yellow pages of the phone directory had revealed it to be the one closest to her home. The conversation left the impression of a very nervous person and one with a great need. I answered her questions and secured her name and address.

Some days later, I stopped by to visit with her. The family had recently moved from another state. The husband was a traveling salesman and left at home was a very lonely and depressed wife. She missed her parents, the house from which they had moved, and the close fellowship of a country church. She did not feel at home in the city. She was pregnant with their fifth child, a baby that the husband did not want. She carried the weight of feeling she should go to church and yet she was not doing so. She wanted to talk. I was willing to listen. I realized she needed friends, and I asked her permission to have some ladies of one of our groups stop by to see her. This pleased her and she readily agreed. But she was so emotionally disturbed that she had to spend some time in a hospital. She now had counseling of pastor and psychiatrist. She also had members of a prayer group with whom she was to become close friends. It was this supportive group that sustained her and finally served as the channel through which she was able to face herself and to find a new lease on life. Here she found love, herself, and God. She regained strength, faith, and self-confidence. Her husband, involved in an affair with a woman in a distant city, realized his responsibilities and broke it off. Their home life improved as they found happiness in a united family.

My counseling efforts were enhanced and enriched because of a group who were not experts, but enthusiasts. They cared for a specific person with a specific problem. They had a special answer—love. They experienced what it means to minister "unto the least of these . . ." This particular couple never became members of our congregation. This was not our goal. Our goal was to help. This help they received in the proper spirit and found each other and themselves. This was reward enough. Counseling on my part became more meaningful because others cared.

Stressing the Importance of Counseling

I have found it helpful to designate at least one specific day each month for counseling. Such emphasis teaches the importance of counseling at any time and at any day or hour, helping the entire congregation to be more aware of the opportunities and importance of pastoral counseling. It frees one entire day for this special interest each month and provides a time for the scheduling of interviews that are not so urgent that they must be considered the moment they become known. It is an opportunity for the pastor to invite individuals to come to see him when he desires to consider some aspect of church life or individual concern.

The laity should be involved in the day of counseling. Prayer is one of the most tangible ways to do this. The early morning hours through late evening can be divided into half-hour periods and members asked to sign when it would be convenient for them to come to the church for prayer. The prayer period can be observed in the nave, chapel, or in a special room prepared for this purpose. Devotional materials, altar setting, Bible, paper for listing prayer requests, and prayer book should be available. Individuals are encouraged to come by themselves or with others. If there are prayer groups comprised of members of the congregation, they can meet at the church on this day. This makes prayer the focal point of congregational life, not a fringe aspect. The pastor will sense definite help through the knowledge that many are in special prayer with him on this day. It will be a help to him as he ministers through counseling to the many or few who may see him on this day or at any other time during the month.

Judicious use of prayer during counseling periods is of value to the pastor. Fortunate is the pastor whose study is accessible to the chapel and/or nave of the church. Frequently, individuals will spend time in the chapel or nave before or following a counseling session. Often these are the most valuable moments. Also, the pastor on occasion may want to go with the person counseled to the nave or chapel for prayer.

Fasting on the Day of Counseling

Fasting is a little-used but available means of spiritual growth. Believers through the centuries have discovered it to be spiritually rewarding and conducive to a fruitful ministry. The monthly day of counseling serves as a time to stress fasting. It is an asset to the devotional life of those who observe the day in fasting; and, for reasons that cannot be explained, it undergirds the effort of pastoral counseling providing an atmosphere of spiritual commitment that is conducive to more effective work. Fasting induces intercessory prayer for all for whom the congregation is responsible, and especially those whom the pastor will counsel on this day. Our Master practiced fasting, and so should we.

Appointments for Counseling

The pastor can minister most effectively if appointments are made by those seeking counseling. This should be done wherever possible. At the same time, the pastor wants individuals to know that he is willing to talk with them at any time. Especially on the day of prayer, fasting, and counseling someone may come to the church for prayer and suddenly decide that he wants to speak to the pastor. He should be encouraged to do so; appointments are not nearly so important as meeting needs.

Prescriptions

The pastor should not hesitate to prescribe for those seeking his counsel. It may be a referral to a medical doctor, social worker, psychiatrist; it may be suggested meditation on passages of Scripture, a book, or magazine; it may be advice to participate in a group. If the prescriptions are written down, it is better for the counselee.

No pastor should assume that he is an expert in all fields and that he can help every person. Neither should he assume that he must always make referrals to other professionals. Professional help has its place. God has given different talents to different men. It is not, however, the entire answer. Even if it were, there are not enough professional counselors to meet all the needs. Those receiving such counseling help must continue to live with others and still need love, understanding, and care or all the professional help is undermined at the foundation.

The pastor must have confidence in God's power as it is extended through human channels. The laity, the professional counselors, pastors, and all other individuals seeking the good of others must work hand in hand to bring wholeness to the ill of body, mind, and spirit.

LOCAL CHURCH PRAYER CALENDAR

The local church prayer calendar is an adaptation of the calendars used successfully for years by various denominations and other religious movements. The Church must practice as well as preach the importance of prayer and the individual. Prayer is not a waste of time, and individuals appreciate being remembered in prayer by others. The entire family of each name appearing on the prayer calendar should be included in one's prayers. This brings a personal touch in the midst of the maze of program and organization. It helps develop and maintain greater personal concern for one another on the part of the members.

Listing of Members

Most members will never have their name appear in the church bulletin or parish letter. The prayer calendar takes care of this matter. At least once a year every member is listed; in smaller churches, names appear several times throughout the year.

One method of listing members is alphabetical. Each month continue with more names, listing three to five names each day. When all names have been listed, begin again.

Another, and more meaningful, method is to list members according to their birthdays. His birthday is always significant to each individual; it is a day on which he loves to be remembered by friends. The remembrance could not only be in prayer, but also with a birthday card. A prayer calendar listing members by birthdate encourages the sending of greetings to one another. Members should be encouraged to do this.

The pastor would find it a blessing both to him and to the parish members if he would send a birthday card to each. He should want to sign each card personally and in some cases add a personal note. Most people receive many cards at Christmas but few on their birthdays. They really appreciate the remembrance of this day by others, and especially by their pastor. In larger churches, volunteers may help the pastor address the cards and mail them. They should be addressed a month in advance. (The date to be mailed should be noted in the upper right-hand corner of the envelope, where the stamp will cover it when it is mailed.) This certainly is a church expense well worth the time and money.

A sentence should appear on each monthly prayer calendar reminding individuals to pray for the family of the members listed. Also, it should be stated that if there is an error as to the date of birth, the individual should call the church office so that correction may be made.

Significant Events

The significant events of a parish should also be listed on the prayer calendar. It keeps prayer for activities from being incidental; it puts first things first.

Also, significant world events, special days, world leaders, and other items of importance should be listed from time to time. Surely the entire congregation should be praying for our President and other world leaders.

Boys in Service

The back of the prayer calendar provides space for printing items of interest and important future events. Since families will keep the calendar throughout the month, wise choice of what should appear here is essential. This section of the prayer calendar is an excellent place to list the names and addresses of those from the congregation who are serving in the armed forces. The congregation should pray for them often and write to them. Failure to do this is a reflection upon the sincerity and depth of a congregation's Christian witness. The men and women in the armed services like personal letters and appreciate mail from the congregation. Some of them may not have been faithful in church school or worship attendance, but they will eagerly read and absorb any letter sent to them. The chances of their appreciating the Church wherever they are based and after they are discharged will be improved.

College Students

Occasionally, the back of the prayer calendar should list the names and addresses of the congregation's college students. They, too, are happy to receive mail from friends at home. The friendly letter is perhaps the finest means of evangelism as far as the college student is concerned.

The names and addresses of missionaries, pastors, and other full-time church workers who have gone forth from the local congregation or who are supported by the congregation should also be listed. This keeps before the parish families all those who are so worthy of prayer and remembrances by mail.

Distribution of the Prayer Calendar

The calendar should be mailed monthly to every family of the congregation. It can be inserted with the regular parish letter or mailed separately. The postal bulk rates apply if over two hundred are mailed at one time.

Extra copies of the prayer calendar should be available at the literature rack and in the church office. Individuals may want a copy to keep with daily devotional materials. Some tack a copy on the family bulletin board. Each child of the Junior, Junior High, and Senior High departments should receive a copy in order to help him to develop a life of prayer, devotion, and concern for others. The cost of extra copies is meager compared to what is accomplished.

Praying for All

Every member of the congregation should appear on the prayer calendar at least once during the year. The Church is a family. A decent family does not exclude one of its members because he may not be living a life that other members approve. In like manner, the Church should always be deeply concerned about both the faithful and the unfaithful. The prayer calendar serves to encourage members to be faithful to all. It serves as an encouragement to the faithful to continue to persevere, and it reminds the unfaithful that they should strive to live the Christian life to the best of their ability.

Prayer for all, by all, is best for all.

CHURCH CARD RACK

Birthday, sympathy, get-well, congratulations, thank-you, graduation, and wedding cards should be easily accessible to members of the congregation. Adequate card racks can be purchased or built and placed in the vestibule or hallway. Commercial card racks can be secured at very reasonable prices. Sometimes, when a store remodels, perfectly good racks can be secured for a minimum investment. Such a rack provides a good display for cards as well as drawer space for storage.

All cards should be reasonably priced. The cards need not be sold at list price, but at a price equal to or only slightly higher than the price paid by the church. The congregation should not seek to make money from this service but to encourage individuals to remember friends and fellow church members with an appropriate card. This is a tangible way to foster the family spirit within a congregation.

A committee should be responsible for maintaining the supply of cards; variety and good taste should guide their selection. Any card supply outlet will be more than happy to supply prices and samples.

The Church needs a shot in the arm in adult education. We have expended much money and time in the Christian education of children and youth. Thank God for the recent realization that an equal emphasis is needed with adults.

There has been a decline in Sunday church school attendance and a greater decline in interest. The few adults who still attend fail to come properly prepared as far as the lesson is concerned, and participation is at a minimum. Often church school quarterlies are left at the church or, if they are taken home, soon lost or forgotten. The average church member knows little about the Bible, his Church's doctrine, or Church government, and in most cases he could not care less.

Interest courses involve the study of books selected by a committee of the local church and offered for a limited period of time; they are available to all regardless of age, sex, or marital status; they feature frequent changes of text and teacher. The creative use of these courses affirms that the Sunday church school need not be the most wasted hour of the week.

A Surprising and Startling Beginning

During the fall of 1957, a few persons in a local congregation expressed interest in Bible study. They were not satisfied with Sunday morning classes. The couple who initiated the idea felt that ten or maybe a dozen people would be interested.

There were two requirements for those who desired to participate. First, every pupil must purchase the text. Second, a test would be given every week.

Anyone over sixteen was welcome to enrol. To the amazement of all, instead of one dozen, there were five dozen who enrolled. The results were spectacular. The class was responsive and loyal. The age span was from sixteen to seventy, and this made little difference. They were all willing to study and work together; the wisdom of age mingled with the enthusiasm of youth.

The results of this effort were astounding. For instance, the couple who spearheaded the effort now serve with their family as foreign missionaries. The sixteen-year-old is now in college preparing for a full-time Church vocation. An older man who had been active in church affairs all his life and a teacher for years came alive in Christ, and his church activity became a joy instead of a drudge.

A couple who attended and applied themselves diligently told their story at the last of the thirteen sessions. Unknown to others of the congregation, they had been having marital problems and were on the verge of a divorce. They read in the church letter about the opportunity for study. The wife was a nonattending member of the church and the husband did not belong or attend. It was thrilling to hear them tell that throughout the course they had been brought to an understanding of themselves and God in a way that they had never before realized. Studying and discussing the Scriptures together had many wonderful side effects for them. Their home was stabilized. They are still together and now both attend church. Their family ties are more precious than ever. They had an opportunity to apply themselves and took advantage of it. Their story thrilled all who heard it.

These examples demonstrate that adults want to learn, and that the Church must give them a chance.

People today are better educated than ever before in our history. They have had more training in reading, writing, and every other aspect of learning. There is a definite increase in the number of adults who are attending night school, vocational school, college, and other institutions of higher learning. It is not uncommon to have a grandmother graduate from college the same year as one of her children or grandchildren. The Church must capitalize on this craving for knowledge on the part of adults. The type of church school activity that has characterized the Church for the past generation does not meet this need.

The Church cannot wait to challenge adults. It is not a matter of how soon we should come up with creative efforts on Sunday morning, but how long we are going to endure what is now being presented and being received by so few. Innovations must not only be sought but also welcomed.

Frequent Questions about Interest Courses

Why interest courses? Cannot the Sunday school movement continue without being rejuvenated? Why must there be change? What is wrong with the present arrangement?

It may be possible for the present church school to find new life in its present format. However, the chances of this happening are remote. The Sunday church school started in the midst of much opposition; it prevailed because it met a need. Thus, most innovations concerning it will be met with opposition. Mr. Raikes started the Sunday school, meeting in the afternoon with the urchins of the street. He taught them to read, write, and do arithmetic. He used the Bible as one of the books to be read and studied. He was violently opposed, mostly by the clergy of his day. Strange but true, we have gone the complete circle. Today, many innovations are opposed violently by lay people while the clergy are striving to try new forms of creative learning. If your church school is really meeting needs and lives are being changed by it, there is no need for change. If not, then serious thought should be given to the following pages.

Three areas of concern regarding interest courses will be considered. First, the effects of these courses upon the Church as a whole; second, what they mean to the teacher and teacher training; and third, the most important of all, what they mean to the pupil.

Interest Courses and the Church

The Church pioneered mass education. Day school, Sunday school, college, and other institutions were started by individuals with deep religious convictions. Their opposition felt education was unnecessary, but these brave and hardy souls triumphed so that all men might learn to read the Word of God. It did not take them long to realize that to be taught adequately other subjects must also be studied. It was not easy for these pioneers in education, but time proved them right. Today, most communities are willingly taxed to provide adequate education for children, youth, and adults. We have discovered that education is not something that we cannot afford, but rather, that lack of education is the most expensive thing in our society.

Since the days when the Church pioneered education and it became a way of life for so many, it has been taken over by state and national governments throughout the world. The missionaries may go to tribes and teach them to read and write, but once a country advances in wealth and knowledge the government steps in and assumes responsibility for education. We are in danger of being outstripped in initiative and creativity by individuals whose main emphasis is not upon Church education. We cannot take a backward step now, but must take a giant stride into tomorrow as far as Church education is concerned. We believe firmly as Christians that education is not complete unless there is an understanding of moral principles, a belief in God and in His Son Jesus Christ, and a belief in the dignity of man.

The typical adult church school class is sterile in content and stymied in growth. Few if any in the class have thought about the lesson or put forth any effort to prepare for the session. They feel no compulsion to prepare. The discussion is of such a general nature that little real learning or practical value exists. It is a pooling of ignorance, not an exchange of ideas.

In spite of this, those who still attend love the class. The church school, which was once suspect, has now become almost sacred in the eyes of some. They almost worship a class or a particular curriculum. No curriculum is sacred and the International Lessons are not God's uniquely chosen instrument.

The Church says that the Bible is the most important book in all the world. I ask you to compare the curricula used in church school to study the Bible with those our children use in school for mathematics, literature, history, and so on. It is hard to convince a teenager that the Church believes the Bible to be the most important book in the world. In school, teenagers study from large, beautiful, and adequately prepared materials; at church they are taught by an untrained and little-prepared teacher using materials far inferior in appearance and content to their schoolbooks. How can they help but feel that the Church is second, third, or even lower in importance. We must emphasize not only through words but also through every resource the importance of Church education. There are so few adults attending the ordinary church school that we have nothing to lose if we start setting significant standards. There is no way to go but up; nothing to lose and everything to gain. We must instruct the interested and trust that in time more will be reached for Christ.

Most people are polite and will not complain about their church's program, but failure to participate should be a message to leaders of the Church. The inactivity is a cry for creativity, content, and challenge. Anything less than this is not worthy of a busy adult's time or effort.

Interest courses offer variety of approach and subject matter. One, we can mix ages. Frequently, classes in churches are divided according to age. There is a young adult class, a middle-aged class, the young marrieds' class, etc. Nowhere else in our society do we ask adults to function under such conditions. The office, the plant, the sales field, and all other areas of work are not categorized merely by age. Why do we do this in the Church?

A person twenty years old may have a deeper appreciation of scriptural truths than someone aged seventy. A person seventy years old has much to contribute to one of seventeen. They should have the privilege of being in the same class if they so desire. Real learning involves imparting wisdom as well as facts. It is ridiculous to believe that individuals are on the same level spiritually because they are of the same age.

More than one person has dropped out of church school because he could not find a class where he felt at home. He was either prematurely gray or had different concerns from others of his age. Also, most adult classes become ingrown and soon reach a spiritual and numerical stalemate.

Mixing the sexes should be done, also. Husband and wife should have the opportunity to attend class together or, if they desire, to take different courses. They may have different interests and needs. They should not be compelled to attend the same class. Couples' classes create even more problems when there has been a divorce or the loss of a mate through death. Where do these people fit as far as the average educational program of most churches is concerned? Entering a specific, limited interest course gives greater freedom for such members and interested friends of the Church.

Another benefit of interest courses is the opportunity to get acquainted with more people. If you are in the same class for a year or a period of years, your friends are in that class. As a church grows, individuals become less acquainted with others, and seldom get to know new members. There is no natural way for them to do so.

Individuals enrolled in interest courses become acquainted with persons they would otherwise have no opportunity of knowing. This is a cross-fertilization of minds and a healthy ingredient to the vitality of any congregation. Just shaking hands and exchanging a few words following worship service cannot accomplish what spending a quarter of a year or more in a class with someone can do as far as getting acquainted is concerned.

Interest courses deepen the spiritual life of the members of the committee who select the books. Whether this committee is comprised of three people or a dozen, these individuals read more books than they ever did before. They learn through searching for something meaningful for the congregation. This is a responsibility beyond the reordering of materials for church school each quarter. There is no creativity or deepening of the spiritual life in simply deciding whether or not to increase or decrease a quarterly order. It takes much time, effort, and imagination to select books that will meet the needs of a congregation. It is a marvelous way to grow in the knowledge and grace of the Lord Jesus, become more firmly grounded in the Word, and have a broader concept of the efforts of the Christian Church in our modern age. There is no substitute for involvement.

Denominations, Council of Churches, interdenominational efforts, and freelance authors are producing fine books today. These purposeful publications should be used by more than a few members of the ladies' association; they should be available to everyone. Interest courses are one way to make them available.

Interest courses provide an excellent way to get good books into the homes of the congregation, because they give a reason for securing and reading good books. Frequent changes of text create new interest. It is so easy to get into a rut. When you study the same type of quarterly year in and year out, the desire and incentive for study wanes.

If one becomes bored with an ordinary class, there certainly is no reason to return to it at a later date; the same thing you left will be there when you return. There may have been a change of teachers, but the quarterly approach is still present. Frequently, when the same material is continually used, the same teacher remains with the class for years. One strength of interest courses for the Church is that if a person enrols in a course and does not like the book being studied, he still may find the quality of the teaching rewarding. Or, if by chance he does not care for the teacher, he may like the book. In the rare instances that a pupil discovers he likes neither the book nor the instructor, he still knows that in a few weeks there will be other classes with different teachers and different material. If variety is the spice of life, no wonder interest courses are so helpful!

Interest Courses and Church Evangelism

What does your church have to offer for those who do not attend Sunday church school? What will it have different to present to them six months or a year from now? If they are not interested now, is there any likelihood they will be later?

The enthusiasm engendered through new courses is more likely to ignite the fire of evangelism. The beginning of a new series of courses is a wonderful opportunity for publicity through the bulletin, parish letter, and from the pulpit to encourage new people to enrol. It is also a tremendous time to call and visit in homes to discuss the courses. It is not easy to maintain a program of evangelistic calling in any congregation. Once a family has been contacted many times, callers are at a loss as to a follow-up. Interest courses offer a reason to at least contact individuals to let them know what is being studied. Experience has shown that some of the most devoted and finest churchmen did not participate in the life of the Church until the opportunity of interest courses was presented to them. It is effective evangelism.

Interest courses indirectly solve and often eliminate many problems that plague congregations. Classes are no longer ends in and by themselves; they are an integral part of the total program. Time and energy are released for other important aspects of congregational life. By the time leaders of a church have attended class, become a class officer, served as a church officer, attended a class social function, and participated in particular projects, there is little time or energy left for involvement and real outreach. Churches are dying that could be dynamic. We live in too dangerous an era to continue in the direction of inertia and ineffectiveness. Interest courses give specific reasons for attending a class and helpful guidance to those who do.

Interest Courses and the Teacher

Many benefits derived from interest courses relate to the teacher. In any class, the teacher always learns the most.

This is one reason why many efforts in church school are contrary to good teaching principles, as they do not give opportunity for a large number of people to become teachers. It is practically impossible to make the necessary adjustments in teacher personnel in many congregations. The Christian education committee is unwilling to remove problem teachers. Members of the class are hesitant to say anything and the committee does not want to offend a loyal member. The teacher hesitates to resign for fear of reflecting on his own ability. The pastor does not want to stick his neck out and cause trouble because he has to live with the teacher and all the members of the class. Thus, the status quo remains.

Regardless of how good a teacher may be, damage is done to the Church when the same person teaches the same adults year after year. Others should have an opportunity to teach and to grow in grace and knowledge. The children's and young people's departments have a different situation. They at least have new pupils every year, but adult classes often have the same pupils attending for years. It is to be expected that these classes become ingrown and the teachers permanent fixtures.

Interest courses establish a terminating date for the class and also for the teacher. The date of the classes is established before the person assumes the position. Individuals are willing to teach if they have a specific subject, text, and number of weeks for the course. Individuals respond enthusiastically when they realize it is Church policy to change teachers and books often, and that no teacher can succeed himself.

Another interesting bonus of interest courses is the preparation on the part of teachers. They realize that individuals have purchased a book and joined the class of their interest. They want to learn something. The teacher feels a responsibility for being well prepared. The following incident is typical. A gentleman had taught the quarterly in a class until he and the class had lost all enthusiasm. He refused to attend teachers' training sessions. One quarter he was asked to lead an interest course. His enthusiasm returned; he sought reference books and studied in depth. Why? Because his pupils were different, interested, and involved; and because he felt the burden of responsibility!

Interest courses enable a teacher to expect more of his pupils. It is not uncommon for a teacher to ask someone in his class for a well-prepared report and get it. Some ask the class to take a test each week and do assigned reading. This naturally develops greater understanding of the Scriptures and spiritual subjects. It makes the Bible live today. A good book is, in a sense, adding another person to the class. Its author speaks to the hearts of everyone present and also to each one as he studies at home.

Secure your teachers months in advance. Give them their text in time to prepare adequately. Remember, every teacher attracts individuals whom others could not reach, just as every teacher repels some. A variety of teachers makes for a broader appeal to a congregation.

Interest courses give a teacher the sense of achievement and purpose that are so often absent in present Church education.

Interest Courses and the Pupil

We have said a great deal about the teacher and interest courses, but the most important person to be considered is the pupil. The best way to assemble a group is to have a common purpose, and yet many Sunday church school classes have no such common specific purpose.

Most classes start with a worthy purpose in mind—to pull the young marrieds together, or the senior citizens, or the men, or the women, or the older unmarried people. This serves a worthy purpose at the moment and perhaps for one, two, three, or ten years. It is almost impossible to assimilate new people into such situations. Those who have attended for years feel at home and love the class but new people have difficulty feeling at home.

Interest courses contribute to continuous creativity and newness. The Church should speak with a prophetic voice and Church education cannot do this without progressive procedures.

Interest courses appeal to a pupil because they add dignity to the study of the Word. The pupil is encouraged when he sees that a course is considered so important that assignments are given, tests presented, and reports expected; and he is stimulated by enthusiastic and prepared teachers. Those enrolled lift their heads high and go forth saying that their church acknowledges the Word of God as basic to all of life, and Christian commitment as the most important thing in the world.

Interest courses make it possible to keep an accurate membership count. Over a period of years the average Sunday church school class has a roll that has grown far beyond the number participating. The officers and attenders of the class do not want to assume the responsibility of deleting members.

Interest courses solve this problem. The class roll is simply those who attend. Since the class is for a limited period of time, this roll is not continued, and thus class membership is kept current. Failure to enrol in any class is simply saying that at the moment an individual is not interested. This is not to say that he is less religious, but that he has chosen not to participate for the quarter. At the same time he is free to renew his participation in a future class of his choice.

Interest courses can be held any time during the week. The question arises, why put emphasis on their being taught on Sunday morning? The answer is simple. If vitality is going to be brought into the life of the Church, some of the things that have become ingrown must be brought to new life. New life on Sunday morning cannot be completely accomplished with new methods during the week. What is gained through the week will be counteracted with the loss on Sunday. It is not that groups should not be held during the week, but the most effective new life movement must involve those who attend on Sunday morning. They must be willing to adjust to the mood of the day, and to the disinterest of most of the members expressed by their lack of participation. Granted, those in the class may be very enthused at times and wonder why there should be any changes. Mature leaders will realize that the Christian commission is to go to those who are not interested and not simply to sit and congratulate one another in a little complimentary club week after week. Some church school classes have become the tail wagging the dog. They are not willing to venture and be creative. They have never learned that believers are called to be servants, not to be served.

These may be harsh words, but the facts are even harsher. We are not meeting the needs of this currently critical period of civilization.

What Should Be Considered?

Each church will have to adjust to its own situation and assess its own problems to determine the content of its interest courses. They certainly should include material that challenges individuals in the study of the Scriptures and in commitment to the Christian life. The content should be of importance and depth. The tests should express Christian conviction with clarity as well as charity. Experience has shown that at least three broad areas should be considered.

1. Scripture study. This involves introduction to the Bible, the Old or New Testament, a specific Gospel or other book of the Bible, a cluster of books of the Bible. It might involve instruction on How to Study and Use the Bible.

2. Practical Christian living. Many persons have no desire simply to study Scripture. They want the Scriptures applied to daily living. They are interested in such areas as the Christian home, applying Christianity to everyday living, making Christ real at work and in one's daily life, meeting the social issues of our day, and relating Scripture to scientific discoveries.

3. Related religious subjects. These are subjects based on the Bible but dealing with areas of Christian life and growth, such as prayer, missions, stewardship, Church and healing, and so on.

There are many approaches to the above three areas and a church will never exhaust the possibilities for variety as there is no limit to the books available.

If a text is repeated, it should not be until at least two years later. At her first meeting, a new member of the curriculum committee insisted that courses of the immediate past be repeated. The wise chairman listened with appreciation, considered the business at hand, and suggested that each member come back the next time with books of interest they may have discovered at the library or in the publishers' catalogs made available to them. The following meeting the person who was so concerned about texts of the past arrived with so many suggestions and so much enthusiasm for the tremendous possibilities available that never again did she stress repeating courses. This is not saying that course repetition should never be done, but be careful not to drift into the snare of neglecting the variety possible today.

Who Can Teach?

A local church frequently feels that it has no one capable of teaching a course on prayer, evangelism, or many other aspects of Church life. This may be true, but already in every church prayer, evangelism, missions, and every other aspect of the Christian life are being taught, although not always effectively. Interest courses help improve the present efforts.

Individuals are not asked to teach because they are experts, but because they are learners along with the rest of the class. The class should understand that teachers and pupils are working together to come to an understanding of the Word of God for this day. Each congregation must challenge individuals to tackle the task of teaching creatively. It will prove to be a source of spiritual growth to them and to those whom they teach.

How to Get Started

So far we have discussed many aspects and characteristics of interest courses and the benefits derived by congregation, teacher, and pupil from them. Now our problem is getting them started in the local congregation.

Congregations should strive to meet today's needs without destroying tried and proved methods. Everyone in any official capacity of the Church education department should be fully informed as to procedures, progress, and desired goals. The Church education committee can submit a questionnaire to the congregation concerning study topics. This will guide the committee's selection of appropriate books and courses. The following letter is suggested for all the families of a congregation.

Date

To All
Church Families

Dear Friends,

We need your help! Our committee is endeavoring to best meet the needs of our congregation in the area of Church education. Would you please indicate below topics which would be of interest to you? Please list your first choice as No. 1, second as No. 2, third as No. 3, etc., from the one with most interest to you to the least with the numbers 1 through 10. If there is an area you would like to consider which is not listed, please write it in the space provided.

Your committee is most interested in your reply. You need not sign your name unless you desire to do so.

Sincerely,
Your Church Education Committee
_____, Chairman

I would be most interested in courses considering the following (number 1 to 10 in descending order of interest):

___How to study and use the Bible
___How to have prayer be more meaningful in my life
___How to apply Christian concepts and practices to everyday living
___How to witness for Christ and His Church
___Roman Catholic and Protestant relationships
___Helps in developing a Christian home
___An introduction to the Bible
___The Church and the healing ministry
___The message of a particular book of the Bible such as the Psalms

___One of the Gospels
___Epistles

Please list below any other topic you feel would be of interest to you and to others of our congregation.

_____

_____

_____

Please return your answered questionnaire to the church office as soon as possible. If other members of your family want to respond to this request of our committee, copies of the questionnaire for their use can be secured at the church office.

The congregational poll will help determine the interests and guide the committee in specific choices of courses. Not only when you first begin interest courses, but also occasionally afterward, the congregation should be polled so that the committee is informed of the people's needs and desires.

General Suggestions

Once the committee has moved in the direction of interest courses, these suggestions might be helpful. Emphasize that this approach serves as a means of evangelism. You can well imagine the benefit derived when individuals are asked to attend a class for a limited period of time. In most cases, when people are asked about the church school, they immediately think of being expected to attend fifty-two Sundays a year. They want to be regular in attendance and a part of a class spirit or else not attend at all, but at the moment they cannot imagine themselves attending every Sunday. A period of thirteen, twenty, or twenty-six weeks seems a more reasonable time to commit oneself.

Interest courses can also use movies, film strips, guest speakers, or art. These classes should receive as diligent attention as the classes that use a text, and involve frequent change of leadership as well as variety of materials used. Changing teachers and materials helps to keep the focus on loyalty to Christ and His Church rather than to a particular class or individual.

If possible, use hardcover books for the courses. They give an appearance of significance. They cost a little more, but they will be used more and become a more permanent part of the lives of the congregation. Church education has been hindered by buying all materials from the church budget, or by asking individuals to buy the cheapest materials available. We worship in fine buildings with wonderful furnishings, and worthwhile and beautiful educational tools should be used.

Hardcover books purchased in quantity can be obtained at reasonable prices. If an appropriate text costs over $3.00 per book, perhaps the church budget could subsidize it. Some churches receive a quarterly offering to help supplement the Church education materials fund. If someone cannot afford the book, certainly the church should assume the cost of the text.

The purchase of the book is very important. Educational materials for Church education classes are often little used. There is a lack of responsibility for them on the part of the individual. Purchased books are seldom lost or left at the church. It means something to people to purchase their own text. (If a husband and wife enrol in the same course, they need purchase only one book.) Individuals bring text and Bible to class and to church. Church in a sense becomes a school, as it ought to be.

Guest teachers can be used for some courses but a congregation should not rely entirely upon imported talent.

Guest leaders can be stimulating, and need feel no compulsion to become a member of a particular church. In many instances, the guest can teach an interest course and still attend worship on Sunday morning in his own church. He should be reimbursed for his time and effort to bring a new voice and approach in areas vital to the Church.

One of the reasons it is difficult to publicize the Church is that so little of importance is going on in it. Interest courses are important and can be publicized with great variety. Good publicity material describing the courses should be prepared for each series. The contents of this promotional material should contain description of topics considered in each of the texts, the stated purpose of each course, how it applies to one's own life, when and how to enrol, a listing of the teachers, the dates that courses will be taught, and the names and phone numbers where one can obtain additional information. The material should be sent to every church member and prospective member several weeks before the courses begin. Interest courses offer opportunity for publicity by phone, personal letters, releases to newspapers and radio stations.

Registration

With advance publicity you can encourage people to register before the classes begin. This gives an indication as to the size of the classes. Those who register ahead are more apt to attend. Classes should be open, however, to new members at any time.

As soon as you know approximately how many members will be in a particular course, you can order the text. Most bookstores refund money on unused books or you may offer the surplus textbooks to others in the congregation. Individuals who are undecided as to which course they will take should have an opportunity to review the various textbooks. People who enjoy reading often purchase texts of several courses. A congregation soon learns the approximate number of books it will need for each class offered.

What about Visitors?

One of the objections to interest courses concerns people visiting the Sunday church school. Where do they go and how would they be interested in what was being offered?

Visitors may attend any of the interest courses. They will not disrupt the class. Even though they will not be coming back, they will gain as much as they would in most existing church school classes. It is easy to say to an individual, "We have a number of courses and would be most happy to have you sit in on the one of your choice." Interest courses create a less awkward position for teacher and visitor than presently exists in most churches. Is it not more awkward to guess or ask an adult's age than to choose a subject of interest?

Family Forums

Interest courses involve all members of a family. It is an exciting adventure for several families to meet regularly for study of the Word. Interested families can meet together at the church, or better still, in one of their homes. There should be no fewer than three nor more than eight families involved in this study. Parents, children, and youth should be together for the study period. The Scriptures, books considered, and group discussion can involve all members of the family. Christians are aware of how difficult it is consistently to have family devotions and even difficult to discuss things of the Spirit with members of one's own family. It is easier to do this when involved with others. The hour of study and discussion can be followed with refreshments and a time of fellowship. This strengthens the relationship of the families. The creative church should come up with many ideas beneficial in this area.

The family forum approach should involve a starting and ending date. In most cases five to ten weeks are sufficient. Never continue without change beyond six months. It is better to end a good thing before it becomes monotonous than to have it die because of staleness.

When to Start Interest Courses

No one can set a definite date for a particular church to begin interest courses, but in most congregations, it can be said, the sooner the better.

A congregation can study and survey for decades, but unless it adopts some plan of action very little happens.

It is not absolutely necessary to do away with present classes to begin interest courses. At the same time, new life and creativity are not gained merely by introducing the study of a book in the present class structure. It cannot be stressed enough that the greatest value of interest courses lies in frequent changes of teachers, texts, and opportunity for all to enrol in the course of their choice, regardless of age, sex, or marital status.

In most congregations the present classes will not be willing, nor will they feel it necessary, to dissolve. To help them and others, it must be stressed that there is no perfect way to run a class or church school program. Those who desire to attend and continue in present classes should have this opportunity. At the same time, they should realize that if some who are now members of the class decide to participate in interest courses it is no reflection upon those so choosing or those who remain in the class. As carefully and tactfully as possible, explanation should be given to the present teachers that if some of their pupils enrol in interest courses it is not necessarily a reflection on their teaching ability. It is simply a fact of life that there is no one way of meeting the needs of every individual over a sustained period of time.

An alternative to a complete revamping of present class structure is to introduce one interest course for a quarter and announce that all interested are welcome to attend. As interest increases, two courses can be offered. A new idea cannot be forced upon a congregation. It must grow into acceptance and enthusiasm.

Only in recent times has the Church in America gotten to the place where it can afford the luxury of teaching only what might be called "spiritual things." To this day on the mission field and certainly in the early beginnings of the Sunday church school, the needs of people were the determining factors in curricula. We dare do no less today. We are not called to continue to do what a few feel is a sacred heritage of the Church, but rather to proclaim the unsearchable riches in Christ Jesus our Lord. We need to use the best and most creative means possible to do this. The Church pioneered education and today must be more daring than ever.

Some General Comments

The greatest opposition to the interest-course approach is usually from individuals who feel it distracts from the Bible. They feel called to study the Bible and nothing else, and leaders must be sympathetic to their views. Nevertheless, time will prove that meaningful interest courses enrich and increase the study of the Bible and do not distract from it.

Few churches are now using the Bible creatively, but individuals coming to understand and realize how the Bible applies to life will be inclined to use it and have it become a part of daily living. Good books are as beneficial as good teachers. A teacher in a church school class expounds his own views to a large extent even though he says he is studying the Bible. If it is only the Bible, why not simply let his pupils read it without comment from him or anyone else? There must be interpretation and application. One may not entirely agree with every application made by an author, but the same thing is true of an application made by a teacher. Pupils gain from both methods if in the spirit of Christ they receive and apply to their hearts the truth imparted and are willing to evaluate such in the light of the Word.

Another question is, what about social times if there are interest courses and people are going from class to class throughout the year?

The social life of the congregation can best be met when the social life committee involves the entire congregation. The social outreach is even increased and made more meaningful.

Shouldn't the base of operation for social times be as broad as that of worship and education? This takes more planning on the part of leaders of the Church but it is more beneficial. The church school class does not need a social activity to maintain its interest in study. A church needs social activities to bring about an acquaintanceship on the part of its members in greater depth and appreciation, which can come only through Christian socializing. Social activities should be planned for the entire congregation and with opportunity for those who so choose to participate in them. When the social life of a congregation becomes identified only with particular groups who meet week after week for study in a church school class, outreach through social events is stymied.

Another question: "What about involving the men?"

One of the biggest values of interest courses is that they involve at greater depth the men of a church. Most present church school classes are so nebulous as to purpose and direction that few men can get enthused about them. When men go shopping, it is for a specific item. They find it, buy it, and go home. This same characteristic carries over in the area of religion. If men have a need, they want that need met. If they want to know something, they want the opportunity to learn it. If there is an area of concern in their life, they want to investigate. Interest courses let them know specifically what is being studied, and when, and how, and for how long.

It is easier to secure men teachers when there are specifics. They operate better in tangible areas. Men work at the drawing board, the assembly line, in sales of particular items, or on other specifics with which they deal every day. Frequently, Church life is involved in things with no conclusions. The same approach and attitudes prevail year after year. Interest courses put an end to this dilemma. Men like them.

No Perfect Plan

In conclusion, it must be said there is no "perfect" plan of Church education and no approach that can be eternally effective. The Gospel may be eternal, but certainly not the efforts of man. After a period of years, interest courses may lose their impact on a congregation. It is then that the committees and leaders must prayerfully and purposefully seek the guidance of the Holy Spirit as to other avenues of approach. There is always an answer, but the answers are not necessarily the ones that have met the needs of the past.

And the answers that seem adequate for the present may not work effectively in the future. Mature leaders will face this fact and be prepared for it.

The answer is Jesus Christ and it is up to us to provide the variety and opportunity to present Him. Let us not fail in the challenge of the crisis of this decade. Congregations must be as daring today as were their frontier forefathers. Our changing culture and our world's Christless condition demand and expect the best of all believers.

KOINONIA

Many have the firm conviction that if the Church expects to bear witness today, it cannot rely on its tomorrows. It must be willing to respond at the points where the Holy Spirit is breaking forth in modern church life. One of the prime points of new life is the experience of koinonia through the worldwide emergence of vital small-group activity. This is deep, diverse, disciplined, and dynamic. It is of God, for His glory, and by His grace. The world is the better because of this phenomenon, and there is new hope for the Church in our generation.

Koinonia is an exciting Greek word that appears approximately twenty times in the New Testament. The King James Version translates it as "fellowship" in Acts 2:42, I Corinthians 1:9, II Corinthians 6:14, 8:4, Galatians 2:9, Philippians 1:5, 2:1, 3:10, I John 1:3, 1:6, 1:7; it is translated as "contributions" in Romans 15:26; "distribution" in II Corinthians 9:13; "communion" in I Corinthians 10:16, II Corinthians 13:14; and "communicate" in Hebrews 13:16.

The emphasis here *is* on fellowship, communion, full relationship to Christ and His Church. To our shame it must be said that many times this sense of fellowship is missing in local churches. A basic understanding of koinonia and what is expected from it is necessary.

The Need for Koinonia

A valid reason for the small-group movement today is that mass evangelism does not meet the need in every individual's life. It serves a purpose, but it is not the only form of evangelism.

Another reason for the small-group movement stems from the very nature of our society. We live in a technological age where there is much emphasis upon *things* but little heed paid to people. The Church, of all institutions, should not yield to this pressure but should endeavor to the best of its ability to maintain the value of each personality. A twenty-minute proclamation by a pastor on Sunday morning cannot possibly minister to each man's need as a person. Individuals must have a chance to meet together in a spirit of unity. They must have an opportunity to do this without intimidation by others, and with the undergirding that a close-knit group can bring. Committed individuals undergirded by others bring meaning to life through Christ the Saviour.

How to Start Koinonia Groups

With so much emphasis on the importance of small groups, the natural question is how to get them started. Most major denominations have good material concerning group dynamics. They have specific and worthwhile guidance for starting and maintaining small groups. These materials are helpful in understanding what can be accomplished through group participation.

A most effective way to introduce a congregation to the

concept of small-group involvement is through the local church weekend koinonia conference. Individuals who have been involved in koinonia are willing to help, and it is best explained by those who have experienced it. To be around individuals who have come to an awareness of Christ and of Christ in others helps novices to gain such insight more quickly. Everyone in any particular congregation will not share in a koinonia experience, but there are those who desire and deserve this opportunity.

The Local Church Koinonia Conference

Local church koinonia conferences stimulate those involved and prove of lasting benefit to a congregation. It has been my privilege in recent years to participate in and to direct a number of these conferences. The last several years have been more spiritually productive in my life and in the lives of people with whom I have had fellowship than at any other time in my ministry.

A number of years ago I spent a great deal of time speaking at banquets, youth rallies, revivals, and other meetings in churches and social groups. I enjoyed this very much and appreciated being asked to do so. But I discovered that little was accomplished. I would challenge, but individuals usually left the way I found them. Throughout a week of special meetings I would preach to the best of my ability. Those present seemed to appreciate my preaching at the moment, but the lasting effect on their lives and mine was minimal. Through a chain of events too complicated to mention here, I was brought to realize how much more I could accomplish when the laity of the church emphasized commitment to Christ. Therefore, over the last number of years, whenever I have been invited to a church I have said that I would come if I could also bring lay people from my church and other churches. Instead of going to speak for a week or two, I would ask to come only for a weekend. I had discovered (to my amazement) that more lasting results were obtained during a weekend with the participation of guest lay leaders than during a week or more of my preaching alone. It may be rather humiliating, but it is true: The Holy Spirit works powerfully through the laity, and often more tangible results are seen from laymen's efforts than from mine.

Each koinonia conference has been memorable. There have always been individuals who had come to Christ and made a commitment. Something special happens when the laity are given an opportunity to reveal what Christ has done for them.

There is no greater privilege than to expose oneself to others who have been greatly moved in the Spirit. There is no greater challenge than an open-door policy; help awaits all willing to be open in all things. This is koinonia, whether it is in the lives of individuals or a congregation.

Pre-conference Planning

A koinonia conference in the local congregation can be introduced in many ways. There are thousands of opportunities to move into deeper experiences in Christ, but most individuals do not take advantage of more than a few of them. If one or two in a church desire real koinonia experience, they will accomplish it.

The better the groundwork is laid for an understanding of koinonia, the more fruitful the results. Those interested should point out the value of small-group activity. Whether combating alcoholism, loneliness, or sin, there is strength in small-group therapy. Group dynamics work in any area of life and should not be neglected in the spiritual.

Attend a Conference

More can be gained through experience than through anything else. A delegation from the congregation can attend a nearby small-group conference to help build up enthusiasm for one by the local congregation. Throughout this period of incubation there should be much prayer on the part of interested individuals, as all efforts should be saturated with the spiritual power derived from prayer. If possible, a few should pray together as well as privately.

Literature

Introducing church members to books and magazines with emphasis on new life in the Church is helpful. The pastor can do much to promote reading material that stresses personal commitment. Pastors are often indifferent to the movement of the Spirit today and unaware of what is taking place in so many different churches. They should be acquainted with fellowship materials and acquaint their congregation with them.

The pastor should not be alienated from the small-group emphasis. Beware of a situation wherein one or more laymen become enthused about small-group work and in their enthusiasm reflect unfairly upon the pastor and others of the congregation. Nothing hinders the weekend koinonia conference more than the pastor's feeling he is being railroaded. The Holy Spirit can work despite the negative attitude of the pastor, but the Spirit's work is so much more effective when the pastor is sympathetic toward parish endeavors.

Someone must spearhead the mechanics and methods of the small-group experience in the local church. This individual must have the determination and willingness to expend much time and effort. If at all possible, he should have participated in at least one previous conference. He should seek guidance and help in a spirit of give-and-take as administrative procedures are followed. When such a dedicated individual arrives on the scene, koinonia will happen.

Action of the Official Board

It is important to get the endorsement of the official governing body of the church for the conference. Leaders should understand what is being asked of them before they are asked to endorse such a proposal.

A respected leader of the congregation can present the details of a conference to the ruling body and answer any questions they may have. A koinonia conference should be presented as one way in which the Spirit of the Lord moves, one way in which the Church ministers to the needs of its individuals, one way new life comes into the congregation. Conferences should never be presented as an answer to all the problems of the Church.

Pre-conference Planning Following Official Decision

Prayer should undergird all efforts. Encourage the reading of books in the field, and subscriptions to such magazines as *Faith at Work*. Select sincere and open-minded people who are willing to go deeper into study for Christ and His Church. Give them an opportunity to get acquainted with what is taking place in other churches and in the lives of other individuals. Frequently, unsuspected sources provide leadership and help for a weekend conference. Do not slight anyone; at the same time, do not coerce anyone.

The Conference Director

As soon as possible after the initial endorsement of the conference by the official board, a conference director should be decided upon. He should be an individual with a warm personality, a sincere spiritual commitment, a deep and genuine love for people, and an understanding of group dynamics, one who is open to God and who has experienced koinonia. He should be acquainted with many people who have participated in conferences, and should be able to recommend individuals whom the local church can contact to help on the weekend. It will be his responsibility to pull the team together in spirit, method, and commitment when they arrive for the conference.

The conference director should introduce to all present at the first meeting the theme, thrust, and goal of the conference. He should be the local church's guide in small-group activity before and following the conference. He should give guidance in practical aspects of the administration of the conference and in resource material. He should assume responsibility for the adjustments necessary in every conference and for the decisions made concerning the team.

A conference director should be chosen six months in advance of the conference, as there is a great amount of work involved in its initiation and implementation. It is folly for a church and director to plan and conduct a conference hurriedly.

Expenses incurred by the conference director should be assumed by the local congregation. They should pay for travel, secretarial expense for both pre- and post-conference correspondence, pulpit supply in the director's home church the Sunday he is away (if the director is a pastor), meals en route to and from the conference, and so on. The director's honorarium should be paid promptly and without embarrassment to him. He should not be asked what he expects to receive; the church should specify an amount and ask the director if it is acceptable.

Financial support for a conference should be handled in such a way that there is no undue pressure as far as offerings are concerned. Offerings may be received, but the local church should be prepared to subsidize the conference if there is less in the offerings than is needed to finance the weekend adequately.

Securing the Team

Beware of having a "professional promoter" serve either as director or team member. The visiting team should be composed of sincere, experienced Christians with a willingness to share. They are human beings all, with human frailties and shortcomings, but they should possess a burning desire to have others know Christ. They are a group not of experts, but of enthusiasts. They are enthused about Christ and His work. Team members are not professionals who know everything about group dynamics; but they are concerned Christians. They have problems like everyone else; yet, they have come to know the Problem Solver.

The conference should be as ecumenical as possible. Often Roman Catholics as well as Protestants can serve as team members. Each will be a voice heralding the Good News.

The visiting team is the key to a successful weekend. They may not be dominant personalities or have tremendous speaking abilities, but they are committed and willing. The team comes with great expectations and they are never disappointed. Every team member is still learning about Christ and His ways. Most of them will not have met each other prior to their arrival for the conference, but their oneness in Christ quickly draws them together.

Lodging for the conference team should be in the homes of the parishioners. Selecting homes is a crucial decision. These guests can make a tremendous impact upon a family. Secure many homes and spread the influence of the visiting team as widely as possible into the homes of inactive as well as active members.

The Friday night meal is usually best served at the church; breakfasts should be at the guest homes. These shared meals are an opportunity for many parishioners to be touched by the lives of team members, and many local families should be involved in providing meals. Every meal in a home is an opportunity to witness for Christ.

Team Expense

The local church should pay the board, travel, and any other incidental expenses incurred by visiting team members in coming to the conference. The planning committee of the local church should understand this and make sure the necessary financial arrangements are made. Attending your conference may be a financial drain on some of the team members. Therefore, it is best if arrangements are so complete that visiting team members can be reimbursed for their expenses before they leave the conference.

Personal Letters

Not only should expenses be paid, but a personal note of thanks should be sent by the local church to every visiting team member. Such notes should be "personal," and not a mimeographed general letter to one and all. Personal letters should be from the pastor and the general chairman and signed by both. Individuals of the local church should also be encouraged to write some of the team members and offer their special thanks for blessings received through their ministry. No one in the church can write to all team members, but everyone in the church should write at least one letter. The more there is an exchange of personal letters to encourage one another, the greater the lasting benefits of a conference.

Securing and Contacting Prospective Team Members

Below is a suggested letter that each local congregation can adapt to its own needs. It should be mailed well in advance of the conference.

Date

Dear [name]:

We are happy to announce that our church is planning a [name chosen by local church] conference for [dates]. It will begin [day and time] and close with the [time] service on [day].

[Name] of [title and city] will be serving as director of our conference. We are praying that you will be able to serve on the team and ask that you please use the enclosed form and self-addressed stamped envelope to let us know whether or not you can come.

We are looking to the Lord for a great conference. We will be praising Him for the team He will be sending into our midst.

Travel and meal expense to and from the conference will be paid to visiting team members.

If you have further questions concerning our conference, please do not hesitate to phone or write us.

Sincerely,
[Signature]
Local Chairman of the Conference
[Signature]
Pastor

The following is a suggested form to be enclosed with the letter of invitation. Those invited to the conference should be asked to reply as soon as possible. At least three weeks before the conference begins, a second letter should be sent to those from whom no reply has been received.

Thank you so much for the invitation to serve on the team at your church on [date].

———I (we) plan to be present. ———I (we) cannot attend.

———Although not able to attend we will be in prayer for your conference.

If you are able to attend please supply the following information and return to us immediately.

Your occupation: HUSBAND————————WIFE————————
We plan to arrive: ———FRI. AFTERNOON ———FRI. EVENING ———SAT. MORNING
Will you be present for the entire conference? ————
If not, when do you plan to leave? ————————

Please list below or on the back of this form any suggestions you may have for the conference.

What is your estimate of the round-trip mileage to the conference? ————————MILES.

SIGNED:————————————————————

ADDRESS:————————————————————

PHONE:————————

DATE THIS INFORMATION WAS MAILED:————————

Pre-conference Local Church Arrangements

Individual involvement in a local church adds to the success of the small-group weekend conference. Avenues of involvement include helping with the addressing of mail and publicity, serving a meal to the guests, telephoning individuals about attending, opening up one's home for small-group meetings, helping with preparation of meals at church, sending thank-you notes following the conference, securing homes in which guests may stay, providing transportation for guests who may come by plane or bus and seeing to it that they get from terminals to the church and to the meetings and activities throughout the conference, praying for the conference, and so on. The more people who come in contact with the guest leaders, the more opportunity there is for the message of the Gospel to take root. The visiting team members look forward with anticipation to the conference, and their enthusiasm will rub off on others. Opportunities for this to take place must be developed to the fullest.

Home Meetings

There should be as many group meetings in homes as possible. Individuals can invite their friends and neighbors to these meetings, which may include anywhere from two to two dozen people. Size is not a measure of success. It is better to have several group meetings even if they are small, than it is to have one or two large groups. Experience has shown that planning does not guarantee the attendance of all who have promised to come. Team members serving as conveners of home meetings should put the host and hostess at ease. The convener has the experience and good sense to know that even if only two people arrive it can still be a meaningful meeting.

The visiting team member who serves as a convener in a home should encourage questions and sharing of experiences, and should present questions to bring forth discussion. Conveners are the catalyst at meetings, not teachers. One of the goals of the home meeting is that it should serve as a guide for the future. It is a demonstration of an effective group. This indirect way of teaching is best.

Publicity

News of the weekend conference should appear in the church bulletin, parish letter, local newspaper, on local radio and TV, bulletin boards, etc. A picture of the director, or of someone on the visiting team, might be used in area newspaper announcements. News releases should be sent to all area newspapers and radio and TV stations. Publicity does not mean that hundreds will attend a local conference, but the mass media should have more news of this type to disseminate, as an encouragement to their readers in this day of sordid stories. A promotional brochure is most helpful. Included in it should be the purpose of the conference, greetings from the director, the conference schedule, suggestions for getting the most out of the conference, information about meals to be served during the conference, explanation of small-group work, listing of the interest groups and their times and topics, homes where the small-group meetings will be held, materials for reading in the area of small-group work, suggestions for those who would like to go deeper into small-group activity, phone numbers of those who could answer questions concerning the conference, names and addresses of the visiting team, and the like. These brochures should be available far enough in advance to be distributed by the local church to other pastors and churches interested in this conference.

The agenda for the conference must be developed ahead of time but at the same time the leader and those participating must be flexible enough to give and take with the movement of the Spirit during the conference. A suggested schedule is as follows:

FRIDAY:

2:00 P.M.   The director arrives.

5:30 P.M.   Dinner for visiting guests and those of the local church whom the committee planning the conference feels should be present. This may be a potluck dinner prepared by the church, or it may be served in a local restaurant with the local church paying for the visitors' meals.

6:45 P.M.   Team meeting involving the visitors and the responsible local leaders.

7:30 P.M.   Public service. A song and a prayer start the activities of the evening. The host pastor should welcome all and introduce the guest director.

7:40 P.M.   Witnessing by visiting team members.

8:30 P.M.   Small-group discussion. Each group should not be fewer than six nor more than twelve in number. Visiting team members convene each group. The witnessing preceding the group discussion should serve as a help to encourage all to share their experiences and reasons why they are attending the conference. Everyone in each group should be given opportunity to participate. Questions such as, what do you expect to receive from this week-end? what is your relationship with God? when did God first become real in your life? set the pace of this discussion.

Quiet time during the group meetings should be used to the greatest advantage. The Holy Spirit speaks whether someone is audibly conversing or not. The convener should explain this. The groups usually begin and end with a time of prayer. The Lord's Prayer, a period of conversational prayer, sentence prayers, silent prayer, or a prayer conducive to group experiences by the convener or member of the group are all meaningful. The convener of the group should be sensitive to the needs of individuals, and if he senses a special need on the part of one person, he should speak to him at greater length following the meeting. Openness is the key. Opportunity is always knocking for depth sharing.

FRIDAY NIGHT (*continued*):

9:45 P.M.   All assemble for closing devotional period.

10:00 P.M.   Visiting team members meet with those with whom they will be spending the night.

SATURDAY:

7:30 A.M.   Men and/or Youth Breakfast.

8:30 A.M.   Team meeting at the church. This is a time of evaluation, prayer, planning for the day's activities, and discussing any problems that may have arisen.

9:30 A.M.   Home meetings.

NOON.   Lunch. Visiting team members eat in the homes of individuals of the parish or at the women's tea, the men's luncheon, etc. A word of caution needs to be said about meals. Members of the local church should not become so involved in meal preparation and doing dishes that they miss the conference. All meals, even those served in the homes, should be kept simple. The witnesses at luncheons should be encouraged to be concise and to the point. Luncheon meetings should never last over an hour and a half. The moderator at the luncheon should keep the session moving and instill confidence and enthusiasm in the team and those attending.

2:00 P.M.   Interest groups at the church for adults and recreation time for youth. Suggested topics for the interest groups: How to pray. The

Church and the healing ministry. How to start and maintain small groups. Faith on the job. Parent and teen relationships. How to know the will of God. Any topics that the congregation feels would be helpful. The interest groups are times of informal dialogue, not professional workshops. Those attending the conference should be encouraged to attend the interest group of his choice.

4:00 P.M.   Free time. If a public healing service is held during the conference, this is an excellent time for it. Those who so desire can attend.

5:30 P.M.   Evening meal.

6:45 P.M.   Team meeting at the church.

7:30 P.M.   Public meeting at the church or group meetings in homes. Some churches may desire to have both, plus a special meeting for youth. If a general meeting is held at the church, further witnessing should be done by visiting team members, to be followed by group discussion. Closing devotional time should be no later than 10:00 P.M.

SUNDAY MORNING:

Team members should be asked to participate in church school classes from junior high through adult. They are not expected to teach the lesson of the day, but to witness of Christ and to answer questions regarding the weekend and their own Christian experiences. Some churches desire to keep all the adults together during the church school hour that they may ask questions of the director and visiting team. The director should speak at the morning worship service, to give a brief scriptural and theological content to the emphasis of small groups. However, lay witnessing should occupy the bulk of the time. The commitment service concluding the worship service should in most cases be in keeping with the tradition of the local church.

Hymns, anthems, etc., should be kept at a minimum to give more time to lay witnessing. For instance, frequently at Sunday worship during the conference the anthem is presented as the offertory.

12:30 P.M. Lunch for visiting team members. This can be served either at the church, in the homes of the parish, or obtained at a restaurant. Each congregation must choose which method is best for them.

2:30 P.M. Closing service at the church. Individuals of the local congregation should be encouraged to speak of what they have gained from the weekend. Visiting team members may make remarks, but they should be kept short and to the point. The emphasis is upon the response from the members of the host church. The director should give guidance and suggestions for the future. He may point out some of the pitfalls and difficulties of the days ahead. The enthusiasm of being present at the conference will not be shared by everyone with whom a person works or lives, because they have not had the benefit of the witness and enthusiasm of the local visiting team. The director should stress that in every conference the visiting team is always faced with the temptation that they have been of little value to the conference. They, too, feel unworthy. He should also emphasize that frequently depression follows a conference, a feeling that it all was just an emotional thing, and other defeating thoughts try to take over. The source of such thoughts should be recognized as coming from the one who would not want anyone helped in the conference. God's help and grace should be sought to dispel these feelings and to grant help for more positive attitudes. Individuals should be encouraged to read materials dealing with new life and Christian honesty and commitment, to seek God's aid in starting or participating in a small group, to attend a small-group conference in another church whenever possible, to ask God's guidance constantly, and so forth.

Some churches desire to conclude their conference with a healing service, Holy Communion, or both. The public healing service is not a prerequisite to a meaningful conference. If done, it is best that clearance for the service be obtained from the official board of the church and proper guidance be given by the director regarding it.

Youth Involvement

A youth team should be invited to the conference, and adults asked to serve as advisers for the youth activities. The visiting youth team should be assigned for lodging and meals to homes where there are other teenagers. Friday night, the youth can attend opening service and meet in their own discussion groups. Their group conveners should understand and love youth and be willing and able to give them opportunity to share without disparaging what they say. Youth should be encouraged to express their doubts as well as their definite convictions.

Saturday morning breakfast gives opportunity for witnessing of youth to youth; it should be followed by group discussion. Saturday afternoon is youth recreation time. Youth frequently prefer this to attending interest groups, although any who desire to go to an interest group should be encouraged to do so. If a healing service is conducted in the late afternoon, the entire youth group should be encouraged to attend.

A Saturday night hootenany is always well received by

youth. This service can be enhanced by a coffeehouse setting, which is often conducive to discussion and witnessing. The coffeehouse setting is accomplished by using small folding tables rather than large dining-hall tables. Decor is limited only by the imagination of the decorating committee.

The youth should have many opportunities for singing throughout the conference. At least one youth should witness at the Sunday morning worship service, and youth attendance at the Sunday afternoon closing service should be stressed.

The Team as Channels

Each visiting team member should be willing to be himself and let others be open toward him. This happens most often when members of the team have an opportunity to meet together for a few minutes, such as at the Friday night team meeting. Each must be willing to communicate quickly and completely; cleared channels are most effective.

The local church will want to expose visiting team members to many people. One objective of the weekend is to have as many as possible hear and become acquainted with the visiting team members. No opportunity for such exposure should be neglected or missed by pastor or people.

Congregational Response

It is obvious that the small-group movement is not the only way the Holy Spirit works; the weekend conference is but one aspect of an exciting Church life. Such a conference does not downgrade programing, missions, stewardship, Church education, and all other aspects of a vital Church. It simply is a concentrated effort in the area of witnessing and depth dialogue. Many churches have discovered that all other areas of their church programs have been strengthened through people communing with God and with one another in this way.

Any church that waits until everyone clamors for small-group activity will never conduct a conference. A church is fortunate if ten per cent of its membership participate in depth. Nonetheless, that ten per cent can influence many. Usually they become the leaders in church administration, teaching, calling, contributing, and leadership education, serve as committee chairmen or members, and so on. Their approach makes church life more vital and vibrant.

Starting a Group

Throughout the conference individuals attending should be challenged to start or participate in small groups. They should be reminded that it only takes two people to start a group, and to maintain a group. Those starting a group must be willing to begin, regardless of what others do, and be willing to continue, regardless of how others react.

There is no mechanical way to program a depth group experience. It is impossible to take the membership and simply divide it into zones and come up with meaningful group dynamics. Groups must be the result of the movement of the Spirit, not mechanical organization.

Helps for the Convener of Groups

The following helps might be useful to the convener of a group during a weekend conference or for beginning and maintaining a group in the local congregation.

First, a convener should briefly introduce himself and

say why he was willing to convene the group. Everyone in the group should then have the opportunity to introduce himself too, and to state his reasons for attending.

After these preliminaries it is good for the convener to share something in his life. This should be brief and to the point. He is then ready to proceed with one or more of the following or other challenging questions: Where do I see Christ in my life today? As far as I am personally concerned, is Christ alive? Do I know about Christ only because of what I have heard or because of what I have experienced? Where do I feel I want and need help at this present moment? What is the greatest need in my life at the moment? The greatest joy? What does the Bible have to say to me in my present situation?

It is wise to have a time of quiet listening following the questions, to enable the Holy Spirit to speak. The convener and group should not fear or neglect quiet times. Sometimes the Holy Spirit works more forcefully during quietude than during conversation.

After this period of quietude, each may respond as he feels led. It is not necessary to go around the circle one after the other, but each should respond as he desires. The convener should see that no one does all the talking and yet that none are deprived of an opportunity to say something. No person should be forced into conversation.

If the convener senses a great need in one of the group he is wise to share at greater depth with this person following the group meeting or at some other time during the conference. The closing moments are good ones to ask members of the group to participate in short personal prayers; they can leave out the formal *Thee*'s and *Thou*'s and make their prayers more personal and pointed. It can be stressed that Christ is present and personally concerned about everyone and every concern of the group. Specific prayer is the aim.

The convener should do as little talking as possible. He shares of himself, but not overly so. He encourages others to express themselves, and to verbalize and articulate their joys, fears, and doubts. The convener's remarks must be pertinent; the experiences must be personal and not just abstractions. The group is not there to debate theology, but to experience Christ. This is not a time of analyzing what is wrong with the Church today, or even what is good about it; it is a time to share experiences of the living Christ. Individuals must see and hear of Christ at work in lives and circumstances today.

The convener can be alert not only for the hungry heart with whom he can talk at greater length, but also for individuals in the group who may have a special ministry to another in the group or at the conference. No convener can meet the needs of everyone. Others can sometimes speak more genuinely to a particular need in a particular individual's life.

Helpful Materials

A weekend conference provides opportunity to distribute materials about group work and Christian growth. Everyone attending should receive a schedule of the conference, a bibliography on small-group work, a copy of *Faith at Work* or some other magazine that deals with personal experiences, guidance for group participants, helps for starting groups, a list of visiting team members with addresses and phone numbers, the location of the discussion groups in the church, addresses of homes in which groups will meet, a list of Saturday afternoon interest groups and where they will meet, a map of the church building and of the city, an evaluation sheet to be filled out following the conference, and any other material that the local church feels would be helpful. These items can be enclosed in a large manila envelope on which the conference schedule and other pertinent information can be mimeographed.

Conference Prayer Partners

A local church can have members serve as prayer partners with the visiting team members. They can write to the team member who will be their prayer partner and tell about themselves, their anticipation of the conference, and personal comments concerning their family. This should be done at least thirty days prior to the conference if possible. The visiting team member should reply by letter to his prayer partner; he should share his concern for the conference and introduce himself and his family. Conference prayer partners are of benefit in many ways, and develop a spirit of prayer for the conference. Also, on his arrival at the conference, the visiting team member will know at least one family in the local church.

Individuals concerned about the conference, but unable to attend, should write to team members, their pastor, or the director in care of the church, mentioning their remembrance of the conference in prayer. This is a great encouragement to those participating. Children, youth, and adults can write. Such letters bless the ones who write as well as those to whom they are written. Some conferences receive dozens of letters and telegrams from friends throughout the nation expressing their prayer concern. The visiting team and local members receive much strength and encouragement from these greetings.

How to Get the Most Out of a Conference

A visiting team member, as well as the participants, will gain more from a conference if all come willing to give and to receive. Visiting teams should participate in as many of the activities of the weekend as possible. Church members need to be reminded that total participation in the conference yields the greatest fruit. Each individual should put forth conscious and considerate effort to become acquainted with others during the conference. The talking should not only be in groups; everyone should try to talk at depth to at least one other person during the weekend. Eyeball-to-eyeball honesty is most productive spiritually.

The shortcomings of a conference should not be permitted to be a stumbling block to blessings. There is no perfect director; there is no perfect weekend. There are no perfect schedules, visiting teams, local churches, or pastors. The conference is most helpful when everyone seeks to understand and to minimize the desire to be understood, when everyone forgives and is willing to be forgiven.

The conference is a demanding time. It is not a weekend of relaxation and escape from the cares and worries of life. It is an intense time of inward searching and outward expression. It is a time of coming into contact with strangers and acquaintances at greater depth. It is an opportunity to learn about and to purchase good resource materials. Thus, to profit most from a conference, one should come to serve and not just to be served, to love and not just to be loved!

Conference Follow-up

Personal letters are important avenues of conference follow-up. The director should write to each of the visiting teams expressing his appreciation for their help, as should the local church general chairman and pastor. Members of the local church should send a letter to those of the visiting team members who were of special help or blessing to them. Team members should write notes of appreciation to the families in whose homes they stayed, or where they ate, or to others who went out of their way to help them. They may want to write to someone to whom they talked at depth or with whom they shared a particular problem. Letters of love and appreciation not only strengthen the one to whom they are written, but the one who writes them as well.

Those of the local church who are especially touched by the conference should endeavor to meet, pray, and seek God's guidance for the future. Some will definitely want to continue to meet in groups and invite others to meet with them. Continuous promotion of books, pamphlets, devotional guides, denominational and interdenominational materials on small-group work will prove helpful. Guidance gained from these sources helps in beginning and maintaining groups.

Another aspect of beginning groups is for the host pastor and members of his church to serve as visiting team members in the future. They will discover that their conference was wonderful, but not nearly as meaningful as the one on which they serve as a team member. Being a team member helps keep alive one's enthusiasm in his own local church. It teaches anew that we gain as we give. The benefits of being a team member of a weekend conference are immeasurable, because it kindles and keeps alive the desire for koinonia experience.

When to Conduct a Conference

There is no perfect season or setting. The Holy Spirit blesses this activity and all will be blessed who move in the direction He is leading. Interested individuals in local congregations should seek God's guidance concerning a conference, and get initial steps under way. It will prove to be an exciting adventure with God and man. Successful conferences have been held in the fall, winter, spring, and summer. Each congregation should come to a decision as to time and place in the confident assurance that God will bless their effort.

THE REGIONAL SMALL-GROUP CONFERENCE

Ecumenically planned and promoted regional conferences for individuals interested in small-group activity can be very fruitful. They serve as occasions of inspiration, information, and instruction for pastors and laity. They complement the efforts in local congregations where small groups exist. Most of the things stressed in the preceding pages are helpful at a regional conference, but there are some aspects that should be different if they are to be most helpful to those attending.

The Director

The person who will direct the regional conference should be secured a year or more in advance; by phone and letter he can give guidance to the planning committee. He should arrive for the conference at least a day ahead of its scheduled opening, in order to meet with the local committee and as many team members as possible. The theme and purposes of the conference should be carefully considered at this time.

The Conference Committee

The chairman of the conference committee should be an interested lay person. He should decide on a director, get out publicity (months ahead of time), provide for room arrangements, and handle all the details of the conference. Efforts should be made to enlist the cooperation of the area churches with this conference, and to encourage their people to attend. Also, the placing of speakers on Sunday morning in the area churches is a valuable part of the work of the director and his committee, and should be planned as far in advance as possible. There are always very capable and well-known individuals attending a regional conference, and local churches should use them to advantage. It is not wise to contact local churches once the conference has started and ask if they want to use a certain person. This should be done weeks or months in advance of the conference. This not only creates a better outreach of personnel attending, but also increases interest on the part of churches in the surrounding area.

Financing the Regional Conference

Some conferences find that charging a registration fee is most advantageous for meeting expenses, while others prefer to emphasize free offerings. Meals should be reasonably priced, and so should all other facilities. Excess money can be used to promote future conferences and other aspects of the small-group emphasis.

The Workshops

Workshops at regional conferences can be of much greater value than they are at local church conferences. Greater effort should be expended to secure authorities in their fields to lead the workshops at regional conferences. This leadership should be sought months in advance. Ideas should be given as to what is expected of a leader, how much time he will have available, and the approximate number that are expected to participate in the workshop. Leaders should make a bibliography available, in order to have books and materials ready for perusal, and to give specific guidance in their area of concern. Promotional material should announce who will be leading the workshops, giving a brief background on each leader. The regional conference should serve the worthy purpose of instructing and inspiring individuals to go deeper into the areas being considered in the workshops. Leaders of workshops should be reimbursed for their travel and effort. In many ways they will be exerting greater influence than the conference director. They will be meeting people in the areas of specific needs and every effort should be put forth to secure the best talent.

Inspiration for Conference in the Local Church

The regional conference should serve as an inspiration for those attending to conduct a small-group conference in their own congregation at the local church level. It should be geared to this end. The use of evaluation sheets, such as the example shown on page 169, and presentations should give individuals an opportunity to indicate their desire to have such a conference. After the conference, a list of all present should be mailed to those who attended. Participants who indicate their desire to serve on a local church team or to serve as a director of a conference in local churches should be shown on this list. An asterisk or other mark would serve to indicate who would do what. An evaluation sheet can be used to secure this information. There are so many churches desiring a conference at the present time that there is lack of leadership. This is not necessarily because the Lord has not raised up enough leaders, but because individuals are not aware of their leadership quality. The regional conference should develop and facilitate the use of leadership.

Publicity

Publicity for the regional conference should be in the mail months in advance, and a follow-up mailing piece should arrive a few weeks before the conference. Complete details concerning the conference should be given in the publicity and every effort made to stress that it is an ecumenical, practical, and relevant event. Publicity should be neatly and attractively printed; money expended to do this is well spent.

The Location of the Regional Conference

The regional conference is usually best suited to a campground, a retreat center, a resort area, or a college campus. This keeps the participants together in comfort and convenience for the entire weekend. It can be held in a church that has adequate facilities for caring for several hundred people, but housing, meals, and many other problems develop in this situation that do not exist when all facilities are a part of the meeting place. Wherever the conference is held, those responsible for the grounds should be fully informed as to events. All aspects of the program should be explained to them and clearance obtained for the use of the facilities and for conducting all services. When the local church building is used, every effort should be made to involve as many as possible of the local congregation in working out the details. The pastor of the church should be fully informed of planning progress and conference procedures.

Regional Conference Evaluation Sheet

I learned of this conference via:

_____newspaper, _____radio, _____pastor, _____conference publicity material, _____friend, _____other.

I attended the workshop_____

    It was excellent_____, helpful_____, of no value_____.

    Comments about your workshop_____

    Do you have a suggestion for a workshop next year?

I purchased books at the conference. Yes_____ No_____

Please list (1–5) which was most helpful to you:

_____witness, _____talk-it-over groups, _____devotions, _____workshops, _____keynote speaker.

Was your reaction to your TOG _____excellent, _____good, _____fair, _____poor.

    Comments:

Would you be willing to serve on a team for a small-group conference in a local church? Yes_____ No_____

Have you served as a team member in a conference before? Yes_____ No_____

Have you ever directed a conference? Yes_____ No_____

Would you be willing to direct one if asked? Yes_____ No_____

What have you gained from this conference?

Is your church interested in having a conference on small groups? Yes_____ No_____

Would you desire someone to come to your church to speak to officials about such a conference? Yes_____ No_____

Would you like information about next year's regional conference? Yes_____ No_____

Will you get the news to others about next year's conference? Yes_____ No_____

NAME:_____

ADDRESS:_____

         street   *state*   *zip code*

TELEPHONE:_____

DENOMINATION:_____CHURCH:_____

(Please Print)

(Use Back of Sheet for Answers if Necessary)

The Conveners of Small Groups

Those who will be convening the small groups should be secured several weeks in advance. Materials sent to them before the conference, giving them guidance and refreshing their minds concerning the leading of small groups, are helpful. The director should meet with conveners often throughout the conference for prayer and for the clearing of any problems that may arise. Conveners should have opportunity to meet together if they serve as a team of two in each group, so as to pray and share together in all honesty, thus preparing their hearts more effectively for the ministry in the groups they convene. Conveners will be willing to share and let others share, to love and to be loved, to give and to take. It is most helpful if they can arrive for the conference the evening before it is scheduled to begin.

The Public Witnesses

Those who witness publicly should do so briefly and stick to the point. Usually, four to eight minutes is sufficient time for a witness to be presented. The goal is not for the witness to tell his entire life history, but simply to zero in on a particular area in his life in which Christ has been real to him. Couples, elderly people, and young people from all walks of life should be used for witnessing. The regional conference committee should strive for variety in personnel and problems each year in the area of witnessing.

It is wise to have one keynote speaker at the regional conference. He should be a well-known personality and one who has an outstanding Christian witness. Thirty to forty minutes is adequate time for such a speaker to present his message.

The printed agenda of the regional conference can very

well include the names of those witnessing at each session, if adequate planning has been done.

A Devotional Leader

The regional conference provides opportunity for at least two devotional study periods. One can be presented Friday night to open the conference and another on Saturday morning before the activities of the day get into full swing. A fine devotional leader should be secured and the announcement of his appointment should be included in the publicity.

Importance of the Regional Conference

The regional conference serves as an opportunity for those interested in small-group work to assemble together, and to invite others to attend the conference. Many first attenders and veterans will be helped in their Christian life or brought to commitment to Christ for the first time. Local churches can have members attend to receive further insights regarding a local conference, because it provides opportunity for fellowship, inspiration, and training which can never be available simply on a local church basis. The regional conference and the local church conference complement each other; they are truly ecumenical and exciting experiences.

THE ANNUAL CONGREGATIONAL MEETING

The format of the average congregational meeting is one of long reports, much discussion, arguments over trifles, and poor attendance. Yet, it should and can be an occasion when the congregation feels accomplishment, unity, and devotion.

The entire church staff should attach prime importance

to the congregational meeting. The date of the meeting should be set in advance, preferably a year ahead. Through every medium of church publicity, every member should be informed and reminded again and again of its importance. Ladies can phone ten or fifteen families, making sure every family receives an invitation. Families should be asked to phone the church for their reservations if they do not receive a call by a hostess. This puts responsibility upon even those whom it is impossible to reach by phone.

It is well to serve a meal at the annual meeting, with the cost considered a normal operating expense. Food can be prepared and served in a manner that suits the local needs and facilities, or it may be catered, served by members of a neighboring church, or obtained at a restaurant. Members should be able to attend and enjoy the meeting from beginning to end; this cannot be done if food must be carried in or local members must cook and clean up afterward.

A large church may discover it is well to have two or more presentations of the congregational program and dinner meetings on different nights (or even a breakfast or noon meeting in addition to the main dinner). This permits all to attend regardless of their work schedule.

Everyone from seventh grade up should be invited to attend the congregational dinner and meeting. Adequate child and nursery care should be provided for the evening. Among ideas for the children's entertainment are movies, games, or a puppet or magic show. The children's program should be announced in advance; their enthusiasm might influence the parents to come to the congregational meeting.

Reports

All annual reports should be mimeographed prior to the meeting. (Chairmen should not cast aspersions on the intelligence of the congregation by reading what has already been written.) The distributed reports of past activities deserve little attention, but time should be taken to answer questions concerning the reports.

Suggested Schedule

6:00 P.M. Dinner
6:50 P.M. Welcome by pastor or general chairman
7:00 P.M. Fellowship singing around the tables. Use familiar songs and choruses led by a good song leader
7:15 P.M. Opportunity for questions concerning past events and reports. Also, brief comments about the present church program booklet which has been placed at each plate
7:30 P.M. The election of officers. Mimeographed ballots to be available to all members
7:40 P.M. The program
8:30 P.M. Singing of "Blest Be the Tie that Binds" and Benediction

In some instances a church will want to close this meaningful meeting with the observance of Holy Communion. If this is done, the service should be conducted around the tables and the devotional period prior to the observance of Communion should be very brief.

Other Suggestions

The use of name tags helps people to get better acquainted. The hostess should prepare a tag for each one at her table and introduce people to one another. Dinner should be served quickly, efficiently, and on time. The agenda should be followed judiciously.

The annual congregational meeting is a good place to distribute the program booklets for the coming year. The total impact is greater here than if booklets are distributed personally to homes; it has the psychological effect of "the entire program for the entire membership."

The hostess should keep a list of those present at her table and give it to the general chairman at the close of the meeting. The day after the meeting an appropriate letter should be sent to all families of the church who were not represented at it. Enclosed with the letter should be a program booklet. Letter and booklet should be sent to absent resident members, nonresident members, those in the armed services, and college students away from home. All on the membership rolls are worthy of consideration; no family should be neglected. A committee and letter for this purpose should be part of the pre-meeting planning.

Presenting the Church's Program

A congregation should capitalize on the phenomenon that people enjoy seeing pictures of themselves, their children, and grandchildren. A program using beautiful slides can keep the congregation enthralled for an hour with no difficulty. Modern techniques of picture and sound make possible a program of almost professional quality. There are always those in a congregation who are experts at photography and tape recording, and they can prepare this part of the program. An effective meeting is well worth the time it takes. Pictures taken of activities throughout the year guide in preparing reports; also, items to be reported help in the selection of pictures. The report should be brief, touching the highlights of the year, and the mimeographed material supplied at the meeting and periodically throughout the year should inform the congregation of program details.

The more people involved in preparing for a meeting, the more important it becomes to them. Enthusiasm is contagious. The natural result is an increased interest in the Lord's work. Throughout the year, activities should be taped and photographed, looking forward to the congregational meeting. This makes it possible to present not only pictures but also actual recordings of classes, children's choirs, adult choirs, portions of a pageant or play, vacation church school closing activities, or any other pertinent activity.

Professionally recorded music, anthems by the adult choir, and the like can be used as background music. Similarly, scenery slides, religious pictures, and so forth at the beginning or end of the program can provide moving experiences. All reports should be properly synchronized with appropriate slides. The person making the report should be shown along with his family. For instance, Mr. Jones, chairman of the worship committee, could begin his report with a picture of his family showing on the screen. He introduces himself, his wife, and their children. This personalizes his report. He proceeds with his report and the pictures that accompany it.

None of the reports should be long, and as many different families as possible should give them. They should be prepared well in advance of recording. They must be concise and yet complete enough to be helpful. The use of too many slides is distracting; either they must be shown too rapidly or the program becomes too long. If a picture is worth a thousand words, an entire volume could not present to a congregation as adequate an interpretation of a church's program as a series of slides with good commentary.

Pictures can also accentuate interest in missionaries who are being supported by the congregation, summer camping, retreats, new members, healing services, small groups, and so on.

The theme and emphasis of the program should vary

from year to year. One year's program may simply be the presentation of the many activities by the different chairmen. The following year may feature two people in purposeful dialogue concerning their church. This program may take the approach of one person questioning the validity of the Church and its interest in people. His questions are answered with explanation of what the Church does and its genuine concern for people. Another approach can be asking families to witness how they have been helped through their church. These personal reports emphasize the area of Church life which has most meaning for an individual. Some are helped through church school classes, others through counseling, worship services, sports events, healing services, small groups, teaching, or any one of a variety of other things. Thus, again the story of the Church is told but with freshness and interest. This type of presentation is moving and vividly portrays the real reason for the Church's activities.

One more example of presenting the congregational story creatively through picture and recording is the approach of a TV documentary. This type of program can be most entertaining and informative to the congregation.

Details Are Important

Creative presentations involve many details: pictures to be taken, individual reports prepared, general outlines readied, publicity, recording of reports, dubbing in background music, and synchronizing of slides and audio portions. This all demands the work and cooperation of pastor and people. The final product should be so well done that parishioners will want to invite prospective members to the meeting. Their guests will get a better picture of their church than in any other way possible.

A suggested timetable for preparing for the congregational meeting follows. The number of weeks or days before the meeting when each aspect should be done or started appear in parentheses.

Begin to formulate the program for the coming year. (*12 weeks*)

Appoint general chairman, secure women to phone and to be hostesses at each table at the congregational meeting and make arrangements for the meal. (*8 weeks*)

Begin preparation of reports. (*6 weeks*)

Publicity about the meeting begins to appear in bulletin and parish letter. (*6 weeks*)

Begin the printing of the annual program booklet. (*4 weeks*)

The meeting of the hostesses. They will be instructed as to whom to call and when, asked to care for table centerpieces, and given instruction on securing names of all who sit at their table or tables. (*4 weeks*)

Slides, taken throughout the year, should be reviewed, and appropriate ones chosen for the program. (*4 weeks*)

Reports recorded. (*10 days*)

Begin phone calls on the part of hostesses for reservations for each family. (*10 days*)

Put all slides in proper order. Music and other prerecorded events put on the completed tape. (*5 days*)

Committees previously secured for this purpose will meet and see that all booklets are mailed to every family who is not represented at the meeting. (*The day following the meeting*)

Announcement in the parish letter or weekly bulletin following the congregational meeting gives a brief report of total attendance, response on the part of those present, thanks to all who made it a success, and the date of next year's congregational meeting. (*As soon as possible*)

THE ANNUAL PROGRAM BOOKLET

In addition to the excellent denominational materials which serve worthy and diverse purposes, the congregation is wise to have its own annual program booklet.

Churches can plan most of their activities a year in advance, and modern means of printing or mimeographing make it possible to prepare an attractive booklet listing them.

The biggest difficulty in preparing an annual program booklet is the preparation and printing of the first one. After that, a church learns by its mistakes, and each year the booklet becomes more complete and functional.

How to Get Started on a Booklet

The official board should approve a committee to be responsible for the preparation of the program booklet. The committee should enlist the help of the entire congregation. Every parish member should have the opportunity to offer suggestions for programing, to criticize the present program, to appraise and evaluate current activities, and to express themselves in general.

All leaders should be involved in the clearing of dates, listing of activities, and suggestions for the future. A questionnaire submitted to the entire congregation is helpful. Only a small percentage take the time to respond, but at least all have the opportunity to do so. All these factors are important if the booklet is going to be meaningful, and if the congregation is going to feel that it is truly "theirs."

What Should Be Included?

The booklet should be a comprehensive presentation of a church's program. A message by the pastor, encouraging the reading and use of the booklet and thanking those involved in its preparation, should preface the booklet.

Committee Analysis

Included will be the important section of an analysis of the different committees and agencies of the church, and a listing of which agency is responsible for what. One of the problems most churches face is not knowing who is responsible for what activity. It is a great timesaver to have the committee responsible for the annual program appraise all committees and agencies of the church and develop understanding of specific responsibilities. This makes it much easier for committees to function as well as being a great help to members of the congregation. Chairmen, committee members, and people are more at ease and more efficient if clear-cut lines of responsibility exist. Committee analysis and listing of responsibilities should become more precise and purposeful each year.

The names and phone numbers of officers, committee members, and members of subcommittees should appear in the booklet. Thus it is important that elections and appointments be made several weeks before the congregational program or fiscal year begins. This gives time for all pertinent information to appear in a program booklet.

Activities and Responsible Committees

Other items that should appear in the booklet are the stated meetings of the church, the times of committee meetings and choir rehearsals, dates of Holy Communion observance, special events, denominational and interdenominational dates of interest to the local church, and a complete list of children's, youth, and adult activities for the year.

The following is a suggested way to list the activities of the year:

DATE	TIME	ACTIVITY	RESPONSIBLE
Jan. 4	7:30 P.M.	Holy Communion	W
Jan. 16–19	8:00 P.M.	Preaching Mission	E

A letter of the alphabet designates each committee. Therefore, the activity calendar shows that on January 4, at 7:30 P.M., Holy Communion will be observed and the worship committee is responsible for it. (The worship committee has W as its key.) January 16–19, beginning each evening at 8:00 P.M., is a preaching mission with E (the evangelism committee) primarily responsible. The key to committees appears in the program booklet preceding the activities calendar.

The activities calendar should be adhered to as faithfully as possible. It is demoralizing for a church constantly to cancel suggested activities. It is far better to list fewer things and actually do them than it is to list many events and cancel half of them. The talent and dedication of the congregation should annually be challenged with as meaningful and complete a program as possible.

Financial Program

The financial program for the coming year should appear in the program booklet. The items in the financial program can be numbered and a paragraph of explanation of each item in the budget included in the booklet. Thus, if the church supports a special missionary project and this is Number 12 in the financial program, on the pages following Number 12 will be a paragraph telling about the family supported on the mission field. These explanatory pages make available to everyone how their church money is being spent.

A statement of the present prevailing philosophy of congregational giving should be in the booklet. Members as well as new attenders should have the current thinking and policy of the church concerning financial support.

The Congregation's Ministry

Several pages are sometimes needed to explain such activities of the congregation as church school, nursery facilities, interest courses, the healing ministry, the church plant, membership requirements, or any other aspect of congregational life that may need clarification in the booklet. The more practical the program booklet, the more it will be used throughout the year.

The names of the new members received, and a record of funerals, weddings, baptisms, members lost during the year, and the like should appear in the booklet. An asterisk can designate non-members receiving the ministry of the church at the time of funerals, weddings, and baptisms.

A section of the book can be used to list those from the local church who have entered, or are planning to enter, full-time church work. Pictures and comments about these individuals serve to inspire and inform others of the congregation. All should be encouraged to pray for and to write these full-time church workers and missionaries.

It is helpful to list guidelines covering the responsibilities of a church; a paragraph concerning the minimum responsibilities of church members is also of value.

Musical Program

An ambitious church may want to list its musical program for the coming year, as it is best to plan music well in advance. Local and guest talent for solos, instrumental numbers, and the date of their participation; dates of the choir cantata; when the different choirs will sing; and other aspects of the musical presentations can be included.

There should be a page providing space for suggestions

and program evaluation. This keeps suggestions current and helps them to be made at the time when events are taking place. Individuals should always feel free to submit suggestions on any aspect of the program.

Church Membership Directory

The directory of church members can be a part of the program booklet. If this is done, the booklet will be used more by families of the congregation. They are more apt to mislay a booklet that has only programing in it. Putting the directory and activities program together assures greater use of both. The name, address, phone number of all members should be included. Some churches include the entire family in the directory; they may add the month and day of wedding anniversary, month and day of birth of husband and wife, and month, day, and year of birth of the children. The following, with anniversary date at the left, is an example of the listing of a family in the directory:

5/20   Doe, John 6/21; Mary 8/17
       Jane*, 10/11/57; Joseph, 8/24/62; Richard, 3/24/67
       248 Shady Drive   478–6242

The inconspicuous line under the M of Mary's name designates that she is not a member; the asterisk beside Jane's name indicates that she is the only child of the family who is a member.

The appearance of the booklet is very important. The use of pictures, although they are a little more expensive, adds a lot. Pictures of the pastor, church building, full-time church workers from the congregation, missionaries supported, secretary, staff members, committees, session, official board, and other groups of interest can be included in the booklet.

The cost of printing may be prohibitive to many congregations, but even a mimeographed effort can be neat and attractive. Electronic stencils can be used for pictures, special headings, and lively illustrations that add sparkle to the booklet.

The booklet pages should not be crowded. If 8½" × 14" paper is used, it can be folded to create an attractive booklet 8½" × 7"; if letter-sized paper is used, pages can be stapled together, although a much neater appearance is gained by using a plastic spiral binding.

Color adds variety. Different colors of paper can be used, as well as different colors of ink. This helps to put the booklet together with pages in the proper order as well as giving more variety and a finer appearance.

Who Should Receive the Booklet?

Every member family and active prospective family should receive a copy of the booklet. Extra copies should be printed to be given to new families coming into the church during the year. A booklet shows that a church is active. It says, "Look what is happening. Join and work with us!" The more specific and comprehensive it is, the more helpful it will be to the congregation.

THE WEEKLY PARISH LETTER

Experience has proved that a weekly parish letter is effective. It increases communication in a church, and the concept of the Christian faith becomes more contagious as the congregation's spirits are lifted. No member family should be shortchanged on the experiences of this spirit.

Modern-day office machinery makes it possible for practically any congregation to mail a regular and neat parish paper, whether it is mimeographed or printed.

What Should Be Included?

The weekly paper should be of interest to the entire congregation. Items may include coming events and details concerning them; a report of immediate past events; a list of hospital patients, funerals, weddings, new members, members lost to other churches; financial reports; a summary of committee and official board actions; the title and Scripture for the next Sunday's sermon; and items of personal interest concerning the community and families of the parish.

Some pastors include the coming Sunday's sermon outline. If desired, the Sunday morning order of worship can also be included; the parish paper then serves as the bulletin as well. Extra copies are produced to distribute on Sunday morning to visitors and to those who forget to bring their copy to worship. This approach develops a greater use of the parish letter on the part of the congregation and is less expensive than producing both bulletin and paper.

It is not necessary to limit a parish letter to one page. A bulk-mail postal permit can be obtained by the congregation from the local post office. Money is saved on postage by this economical mailing of the parish paper.

Tracts and other promotional materials can be enclosed with weekly mailings. Ingenuity and experience should disclose much helpful material that can be distributed to the congregation throughout the year by way of the parish paper. Every denomination, as well as many companies and community agencies, provides free or nominally priced material that can be enclosed with the parish letter. Each major committee should be responsible for inserts throughout the year. One of the committees should establish a schedule for the enclosures and see that it is followed. The following is a suggested two-month schedule; the procedure can be adapted easily for an entire year. Enclosures should be secured well in advance of the mailing date.

Schedule of Mailing of Enclosures

DATE	RESPONSIBLE COMMITTEE	MATERIAL SUGGESTED
Jan. 5	Faith	Tract: "Music and the Congregation"
Jan. 12	Citizenship	Leaflet: "YMCA Week"
Jan. 19	Faith	Tract: "Why I Attend Church"
Jan. 26	Fellowship	Tract: "The Local Church Ministry to Those in the Armed Services"
Feb. 3	Witness	The complete financial report of the year
Feb. 10	Administration	Printed brochure of Lenten Programs
Feb. 17	Christian Education	Tract: "Why I Teach"
Feb. 24	Faith	Tract: " Why a Scientist Believes in God"
Mar. 3	Stewardship and Interpretation	Tract: "Why I Tithe"

Each week the names of the visitors in worship can be listed. A copy of this parish paper can be sent to all visitors, along with a letter of welcome from the church. This means much to the member families who have had relatives as visitors as well as to the visitors themselves, and is good public relations on the part of any church. It is another good reason why a church should secure accurate registration of those attending the worship service.

Who Publishes the Weekly Letter?

Some churches have paid staff to publish their parish weekly. Most churches discover capable volunteers willing to do the work. Volunteers can secure the news, edit, type stencils, mimeograph, fold, staple, address, and mail the paper each week. This saves the congregation money, but more important it is good for those who do it. There is nothing that does a member more good than purposeful responsibility in his church. Members need to be intimately involved in the life of their church, and volunteer office help is one of the finest ways they can show their appreciation for what their church means to them.

Pastor's Paragraph

One final word about the weekly paper. The pastor should feel free to use this medium for relating his own concerns. He can utilize a paragraph or two each week to impart a philosophy of church life or practical Christian living. His and other efforts should be to keep the items in the parish paper current, personal, and purposeful.

Who Receives the Letter?

Every resident member, nonresident member, and prospective member will find the parish paper interesting and helpful. Those in the armed services and college are grateful for a parish that keeps them posted on the activities of the home congregation. Frequently, members assume the expense of the parish paper's being mailed to their parents, to a brother or sister, or to other friends. Wide distribution of the paper is practical; once the original prints are prepared, there is little cost involved in producing extra copies.

THE SPIRITUAL HEALING MINISTRY

Jesus came that we might have more abundant life. This consists of health in *body*, *mind*, and *soul*, because Jesus ministers to the whole man. The wholeness He wished and imparted makes possible Peace, Joy, and Love. Thus, His was and is a ministry of healing.

The healing ministry of the Church through the ages has suffered extreme abuses, and because of this many congregations neglect it. Fringe groups have capitalized on this failure of the Institutional Church to meet the needs of individuals in this area.

There is much misunderstanding concerning healing services. Many pastors and lay people are reluctant to launch into something not generally practiced by congregations. Nevertheless, simply because the Church has not practiced and promoted the public spiritual healing services formally is no sign that no healing has occurred. God heals in spite of the lack of healing emphasis in the Church.

The public healing service forcefully reminds us that all healing is of God; He is the Healer whether a person is an atheist or a devoted believer. This point is taught most effectively through a public healing service. Individuals may pray, but God heals.

Reasons for the Healing Ministry

There is a biblical basis for the spiritual healing ministry. We are commanded to go into the world not only to teach and to preach, but also to heal.

The Gospels and the Book of Acts record many healings on the part of Christ and His followers. Perhaps more people have come to the Lord through healing than through suffering. The Lord knew that healing of body, soul, and spirit was necessary. He did not put undue demands on those whom He healed. He was God, and God heals.

Not only do we have the biblical exhortation, but we have evidence from many congregations of the value of the spiritual healing ministry. Hundreds are being blessed in every way through their emphasis upon the healing ministry of the Church. Their encouragement is a call to all congregations to venture forth on this exciting journey. We are on the threshold of the Church's greatest day, and pastors and laity alike should be interested in the healing ministry. Every church should realize this awakening and be willing to be a part of it. Great things are accomplished as one senses the Christian revolution of this century and moves accordingly. Awakening cannot be denied; therefore, let us not delay being a part of it.

Another reason for the emphasis of the healing ministry is that it is God's will. It is no more God's will that individuals be ill than that they be lost. We admit readily that, because of man's ignorance, because of his frailties as a human being, and because of the nature of our world, there is much illness and suffering.

I can believe that God can ultimately be glorified even from suffering. And, I can also believe that, because of His permissive will in our lives, we can get into trouble. But, I cannot believe that God wills that a little child die of cancer, or that men die on the battlefields. These deaths result from sin—man's sin—from ignorance and human frailties. The Bible says that God is not willing that any perish. In like manner, He is not willing that any be ill. Many are lost, but not because He wills it. It is true that many times illness draws believers closer to God and demonstrates that life is frail and finite. But even death, which is the last enemy, is conquered by God. Even that which climaxes our destruction turns out to be the crowning point of our deliverance. God used death to His glory. We certainly are warping Scripture and settling for less than necessary when we say that everything that happens is God's will. This is inconceivable to me and a misconstruing of Scripture. God may use all things to His glory, but He certainly does not choose the worst for us.

There are billions of dollars spent every year in health and accident insurance, hospitals, doctors, nurses, and the like. Are all these efforts contrary to God's will? If so, then should not believers stay home from hospitals and endure all physical afflictions?

If healing is not God's will, then doctors are the grossest of sinners and our hospitals dens of iniquity. On the contrary, our doctors are used of God as ministers of mercy and our hospitals are places blessed of Him and used to His glory. Let us dispel from our minds the thought that everything that happens in the area of illness is God's will. Let us rather accept and proclaim that healing is God's will and that congregations should be about their Father's business.

When a church starts a public healing service it is not a confession of weakness, but of faith. We have not done all we possibly can in the area of healing until we have sought the best medical help available, until we have prayed and put our faith in the Lord, and until we have prayed with and have been prayed for by others. There is nothing more we can do, but if we fall short in any one of these areas we have not done everything we can insofar as healing is concerned. Scripture, common sense, the direct commands of the Lord, and the experiences of many churches call us to a ministry of a public spiritual healing service.

The Healing Ministry Emphasis

God is concerned about the whole man. The healing ministry is maintained for all physical, emotional, and spiritual needs. Jesus Christ came to make us whole in spirit and in body. The Gospels support the fact that He healed in body so that individuals might realize that He could heal the soul. At the same time, He gave emphasis to the sins of the soul being forgiven so a person might be in better physical health.

The local congregation does not have the spectacular approach of the itinerant evangelist who comes to town for a week or two to stress the healing ministry. Local congregational work is a steady grind. Their healing service is not always an occasion for the spectacular, but an accumulative ministry. Its effects are felt throughout the entire congregation over a period of months and years. If we keep in mind that healing involves the whole man, then healing services will not fall prey to overemphasis on physical healing.

How to Conduct the Service

A simple worship service is the best setting for a continuous healing ministry. Hymns, liturgy, and special music during the laying on of hands can be used effectively.

The observance of Holy Communion and/or anointing with oil may be a part of the service. Most services involve only the laying on of hands and prayer for those who come forward either for themselves or others. There should be a period of silent or audible prayer in behalf of submitted requests.

Before the closing of the service, individuals are invited to come and kneel or stand for prayer. The pastor or the person in charge places his hands on the individual's head and offers a prayer in behalf of his needs and the needs of those for whom he is praying. A slip of paper can be given to each attendant for presenting prayer requests. This enables the one who is laying on hands to be specific in his prayers. Often it is very helpful to the supplicant to list his specific needs. It focuses spiritual power on these areas of concern.

As many people as possible of the congregation should be involved in the healing ministry. Music, for instance, not only adds to the service, but also serves as a way to involve others meaningfully. The committee responsible for other worship services should be responsible for the service of healing.

When to Hold the Healing Service

The hour and night of the service varies with each individual church. One congregation meets Sunday nights at 9:00 in the church parlor, another meets at 7:30 on Wednesday night with the service held in the chapel. Other services are held in the morning. Some churches precede the service with a family meal. Each church must decide for itself on the when and the how. The important factor is that once healing services are started, they should continue. Even if only a few attend, regular services should be maintained, and if at all possible on a weekly basis. If the pastor is away on a particular night, a guest speaker who has had experience in this field should be asked to conduct the service. Elders or other leaders in the local church should be trained to assume responsibility in the healing service and to conduct it at the request of the pastor.

There is no one and only way to conduct a healing service. Each local congregation must catch the spirit of the spiritual healing movement and follow the leading of the Spirit for its own situation. The mechanics are not nearly so important as the spirit and commitment of those participating.

The healing service should be seen in the light of the entire congregation. The individuals who are in charge of the corporate worship service should be led to understand that they are responsible for the worship service at the healing service. All the influence of the leaders of the congregation should be behind it.

Discussion following the service of healing is helpful even if this is done only occasionally. Refreshments may be served, during which time individuals have an opportunity to talk with one another and discuss questions and victories, and to claim promises in the Lord.

Individuals should be encouraged to bring their prayer requests to the healing services. Many congregations provide forms on which to list them. Occasionally, a prayer request form can be mailed in each parish letter. Not every family will use it, but it calls attention to the prayer ministry of the Church. Whatever the need, individuals should unite in prayer for it. The healing service is a prayer time with a deeper concern than just physical illness. Whatever the need of the congregation—revival, spiritual emphasis week, Christmas program, choir cantata, financial need or campaign—it is worthy of prayer. Frequently we pray only when we are in trouble, and other areas of life are neglected. The emphasis of the congregation through the healing ministry is that prayer should precede every project and undergird the entire program.

The Prayer Box

An attractive prayer box conveniently located in a church invites individuals to submit prayer requests. The pastor should call attention to the prayer box frequently, and it should be mentioned in the bulletin and parish paper. The congregation needs encouragement and instruction in order to realize the power and value of prayer. Prayer request forms or any piece of paper can be used to submit requests or to report blessings.

Prelude to Programing

The healing service can serve very effectively as a devotional prelude to various meetings of the congregation. Committees are more efficient, and frequently achieve more in less time, when they are preceded by a devotional period such as the healing service. Every activity is worthy of being undergirded by prayer. The prayer pace set by the chairmen will determine to a large extent how many members of committees and other groups feel a corporate worship experience, previous to its meeting, is important.

Leaders need to act in practice as well as say in word that they believe in the power of prayer, that prayer is not a waste of time. Meetings preceded by a healing service are a tangible way of affirming this faith.

Intercessory Prayer

The intercessory prayer period can involve one or more audible prayers or a period of silent prayer. Frequently it is good to mention by first name only individuals for whom special prayer is being offered, as well as to solicit intercessory prayer for specific needs of the Church, the community, and the world. Individuals can submit requests to be used not only at the healing service, but also in prayer groups and private devotions.

How to Introduce the Concept of Healing

The groundwork must be carefully laid for an effective healing ministry. The following guidelines may prove helpful.

First, secure written materials relating to the healing ministry. Magazines and books should be made available to the pastor and people, especially to those individuals who show a particular interest in this area. Those inclined toward the healing ministry will seek to be highly informed.

Second, it is helpful to have members attend healing services at other churches. They will appreciate these services and have an opportunity to talk to members of another congregation about what the healing ministry has meant to their church.

Third, encourage members to attend conferences on the healing ministry. There are a number of these now being held throughout the nation. Two of the more widely known are the Ecumenical Healing Conference in Ohio, and the Annual Meeting of the Order of St. Luke at St. Stephen's Episcopal Church in Philadelphia, Pennsylvania. The local church should assume the expenses each year for one or more of its members to attend such a conference. The pastor should also attend one every year or two, to keep abreast of developments in this field.

Fourth, another avenue to be pursued is the teaching of a course on the healing ministry. This can be done on Sunday morning, Sunday night, or any weekday. Individuals will find them interesting, inspirational, and informative.

Fifth, a congregation can invite individuals who have had experience in the healing ministry to their church. They can explain some of the strengths and blessings, pitfalls and problems, mechanics and methods involved in beginning and continuing the healing ministry. They can give guidance in the conducting of services and answer questions. They can conduct a healing service.

Publicity

It is important that the healing ministry be kept before the congregation as much as any other important aspect of Church life. Certainly one would not overlook the weekly bulletin, announcements from the pulpit by the pastor, parish letter, bulletin boards, local newspaper weekly announcement of church services, reports by members attending conferences, occasional parish letter inserts of tracts or pamphlets about the healing ministry, sermons, and so forth.

The publicity should not only invite people to attend, but should attempt to point out how valuable healing services are to a church. It is well on occasion to share with the whole congregation through the parish letter or at Sunday morning worship a personal witness of what the healing service has meant to some particular individual. This helps more than anything else to demonstrate the value of such a service. It should be stressed that it is an opportunity as well as a sacred responsibility to pray often and much for others. The healing service sharpens this concern.

The local church will want its healing service listed in *Sharing* magazine. This list is an encouragement to those who have not started a healing service, and a guide for anyone who may be traveling and desire to attend a healing service.

Worthy results of the healing ministry may be shared through articles in one's denominational magazine. An article may spring from the fact that someone has been particularly helped and his story is of interest to the Church at large, or perhaps a congregation has felt a new depth of religious commitment and prayer life through the healing ministry. If individuals from one church have gone to other congregations to speak in the area of the healing ministry, this is a worthy news item.

Spiritual Healing Ministry Sunday

Further support and enthusiasm can be engendered through an annual Spiritual Healing Ministry Sunday in the local church. At this time guest leaders can be invited to present the message at morning worship, teach church school classes, conduct afternoon seminars, conduct a healing service Sunday evening, and so on. Every age, from the youngest to the oldest, needs to receive instruction concerning the healing ministry.

A different theme can be chosen for each year, and talks and materials can be presented in keeping with the theme. The spiritual healing ministry should be an effort of the entire congregation, not just a small segment of it.

A Healing Conference

The local congregation may desire to sponsor a healing conference. This could be held over several days or on a weekend. It could be held in conjunction with Spiritual Healing Ministry Sunday. A special invitation to this conference should be extended to the pastors, physicians, psychiatrists, and nurses of the area. Several churches could cooperate and sponsor an ecumenical conference. Arrangements could be made to house those attending from a distance. Families of the cooperating congregations could house the visitors to keep cost at a minimum for all. The conference should be planned well in advance and director and guest speakers scheduled far ahead, in order for them to prepare adequately.

Adequate advance publicity is also important. Registration at least two weeks in advance should be required from those desiring lodging during the conference.

Finances

The financing of the healing ministry can be done in several ways. Some churches have discovered it is well to place an offering plate near the door at each weekly healing service. Others have special envelopes available for support of the program. The offerings can be used to underwrite programs on Spiritual Healing Ministry Sunday; for conferences and seminars; for obtaining good books, pamphlets, and tracts in the area of prayer, devotional life, and healing. Also, offerings can be used to print spiritual healing sermons, and to mimeograph or print information for distribution to the entire congregation. In some congregations, offerings serve as a source to send individuals to healing conferences and other places where they can learn more about the healing ministry. The local budget should subsidize the healing ministry efforts when offerings fail to meet financial needs.

Special effort should be expended to involve physicians and others in the medical profession in the healing ministry. It is obvious that every doctor is not enthused about the Church and will not be enthused about the healing ministry. However, there are those who could be of great help in furthering this cause. Doctors, dentists, physiologists, psychiatrists, and others of the medical field are becoming more concerned than ever that the Church come into its own in the healing ministry. The Church in no way is in competition or opposition to the medical profession. It encourages the best use of all available medical guidance and help. Nevertheless, it is saying that there is more to this life than pills and shots. It is saying that a doctor's work becomes more effective when vital faith is a part of his patient's life. It is saying that a doctor himself becomes more effective when vital faith is a part of his life, when he realizes anew each day that although he treats, God heals.

When to Begin the Healing Service

The basic question is, are you willing to start? If you are a pastor, dare to lead your people. If you are a lay person, dare to challenge your pastor, and together go forward in the healing ministry.

It can be debated at length whether or not the time is right for the local congregation to begin conducting a public healing service. There is no perfect and complete answer to this problem. I have been privileged to speak to clergy and laity in many denominations regarding the blessings, pitfalls, and mechanics of the healing ministry. The preponderance of them have reacted with "Our people are not quite ready for this." To our shame, although the Church has existed for nearly two thousand years, most congregations are not quite ready in many areas—complete stewardship commitment, a sensible program of evangelism, worship services that speak to the heart, or public healing services.

I do not want to say that every congregation should plunge blindly into a program of a public healing ministry. I cannot answer for a particular congregation; but I can say that, in some instances, ten years from now will be no different—that is, some churches will still be discussing, investigating, studying, praying for guidance, attending seminars, and conferences to decide whether or not there should be a public healing service in their local church. If lay people and pastors wait until everyone in their church is convinced of the validity of the healing ministry, they will never start. This is illustrated by the fact that if any church waited until all its members showed up at a morning worship service, they would never open the doors on a Sunday morning. If they waited until only half of their members showed up, few churches would experience corporate worship on any given Sunday, including Easter. If Paul had waited until all the pagans pleaded for the power of the Gospel in their lives, he never would have proclaimed the riches of the Redeemer.

Much time can be spent laying the foundation for an event and then moving forward from the findings. There is the other side of the coin—where the event takes place and you learn as you go along. In most churches, the latter approach is the best. It is simply true that, when something happens, you learn! How many would be married, and have children, if they had known all about it before the event took place? I took child psychology in college, but, believe me, you cannot put in a book what God puts into a little life. I knew some of the aspects of personality development, but I learned a great deal more the first week after a little girl blessed our home. I have learned more from her than I did studying psychology and writing term papers concerning child development.

This is not to minimize education, but simply to say that education without experience leads only to untried book knowledge. Experience without education and instruction leads only to feelings without adequate foundation. Christian creativity blends experience with education; education with experience.

As long as we say we are not quite ready, we can never be blamed for failing. As long as a person is in preparation, he cannot be held responsible for what he is not doing. In a spirit of prayer, unity, and dedication, the congregation should seek to go forward in the Spirit of the Lord.

No pastor or layman can claim to know all about God and His ways. At the same time no one can say he is really trusting the Lord until he has made a venture by faith, and discovered the joy of adventures beyond oneself as found in Christ.

We know not the end of what we begin, but we know Him who is the beginning and the end. We know not what blessings He has in store, but we know He has many blessings to bestow upon us. We know not what opposition we shall encounter, but we know what inner strength we have found. We do not choose to look back and become a pillar of salt, but to look ahead and to be the salt of the earth. Thus, looking unto Jesus, the Author and Finisher of our Faith, we worship, praise, and trust Him.